Black Theology
in Dialogue

Books by J. Deotis Roberts
Published by The Westminster Press

Black Theology in Dialogue

Roots of a Black Future: Family and Church

A Black Political Theology

Liberation and Reconciliation: A Black Theology

Black Theology
in Dialogue

J. Deotis Roberts

The Westminster Press
Philadelphia

Scripture quotations from the Revised Standard Version of the Bible are copyrighted 1946, 1952, © 1971, 1973 by the Division of Christian Education of the National Council of the Churches of Christ in the U.S.A. and are used by permission.

Book design by Gene Harris

First edition

Published by The Westminster Press®
Philadelphia, Pennsylvania

PRINTED IN THE UNITED STATES OF AMERICA

9 8 7 6 5 4 3 2 1

Library of Congress Cataloging-in-Publication Data

Roberts, J. Deotis (James Deotis), 1927–
  Black theology in dialogue.

  Includes index.
  1. Black theology. I. Title.
BT82.7.R579 1987   230'.08996   86-15665
ISBN 0-664-24022-4 (pbk.)

Contents

Preface

Black theology has come of age. It is now a dialogue partner with theological developments around the world. This is as it should be. The experience of black people in the First World puts us in contact with the entire human family. We are Afro-Americans. The roots of our heritage are in the Third World. People of African descent are present all across the southern hemisphere, especially in the Caribbean and in Latin America. We share much in worldview with Asian peoples. But having lived for several hundred years in the West, Afro-Americans have been greatly influenced by Euro-American culture and thought as well.

The discussion in this volume gathers up all these affinities. The focus of this book is consciously cross-cultural. Black theology is a dialogue partner with theological developments worldwide. We have also been aware of the need to develop a strong theological ethic and express pastoral concerns within our own nation. In sum, black theology is presented here as a bridge-building enterprise and as a project with great promise.

Various disciplines have been used as a resource for this theological expression. Insights from metaphysics, moral philosophy, the history of religions, the behavioral sciences, and biblical interpretation have been used in the development of a contextual framework for the doing of theology.

The insights of this book have been forged in the context of dialogue over a period of years, and I am grateful to colleagues and students who have engaged my thoughts during this time. The first chapter is an attempt to provide an outlook for the book. It is my view that contextualization is an appropriate methodological stance for black theology. In chapter 2, I continue the exploration of African roots introduced in my *Roots of a Black Future.* In that work I was more concerned about the relationship of church and family in the black tradition as a basis for theological construction. Here I am more concerned about method and sources. Chapter 3 was first prepared for a lecture in 1977 at the University of Tübingen with Professor Jürgen Moltmann as my host. I remain grateful to him and to Professor Martin Hengel, then dean of the Protestant Theological Faculty, for their hospitality and support. The chapter developed more immediately from a seminar paper presented in the context of the International Association for the History of Religions, meeting at the University of Sydney. I wish to thank scholars attending the session on comparative and phenomenological studies for their patience and insights.

Chapters 4 and 5 are in the nature of constructive theology relating the insights of black liberation theology to reflections on Jesus and the church and the Holy Spirit in relation to liberation. The subject matter of chapter 5 was first presented in a consultation on the historic faith called at the School of Theology of Virginia Union University by the National Council of Churches' Commission on Faith and Order. The purpose of that meeting was to have input from black church leaders and theologians on the historic confession of Christianity. This essay appeared in the October 1985 issue of *Mid-Stream: An Ecumenical Journal* (24[4]:398–410), published by the Council on Christian Unity, Indianapolis, Indiana, and is included here by permission.

Chapters 6, 7, and 8 were first presented as a series of lectures at Brite Divinity School of Texas Christian University. I wish to express thanks to Dean Jack Suggs, his faculty colleagues, and ministers of the Christian Church for their hospitality and fruitful dialogue. They afforded the opportunity to begin reflections on the relationship between theology and ethics that resulted in these chapters. Further refinement came from additional discussions on these matters with ministers and theologians in Atlanta and the Bahamas. Chapter 9 originated in an invitation to present a paper for a session of the New Ecumenical Association in Seoul, Korea, during the summer of 1984. I am grateful for the refinement resulting from conversations among colleagues. Students in a seminar on theodicy at Eastern Baptist Theological Seminary have contributed more than they can ever know to the final statement in this chapter.

Chapter 10 takes up the process of dialogue between black theology and other liberation theologies. The two programs I selected as dialogue partners are not the usual ones. Jewish liberation theology and Minjung theology are excellent examples for our purpose. I argue that black theology has come of age and is ready to participate in any theological conversation anywhere in the world. The discussion on Jewish liberation theology was first presented as a response to Marc Ellis' provocative paper on Jewish liberation theology, produced for Theology in the Americas. My response was published in 1985 in *Doing Theology in the United States* (vol. 1, no. 1, pp. 24–26) and is included here by permission. The discussion on Minjung theology was first presented in the American Academy of Religion section on Korean religion, meeting at Anaheim, California, November 22–27, 1985. I am grateful that this setting provided me with opportunities for dialogue with Dr. Yung Lee and Dr. David Shuh, Koreans who are engaged in this theological movement.

Chapter 11 gathers up all that has been presented in this volume but also looks to the future. I describe what I see as a crossroads situation and assess what seem to be priorities for the future agenda of black theology. Those who work in this area have a vision of what should be done, but there is a great need for others to join us if the goals set forth are ever to be realized.

As always my wife, Elizabeth, and my three daughters, Charmaine, Carlita, and Kristina, have provided their affection and encouragement. They have tolerated my absence during much travel and study and they have been patient when they had every reason to be demanding of my time and attention. To them I owe a great debt of thanks. To Dean Manfred Brauch, who has brought the support of his office and staff to the preparation of this book, and to Ruth Fox, for her tireless effort in typing the manuscript, I express my thanks. Whatever shortcomings may still exist are my own responsibility. If this study inspires others to be about the task set forth and the human understanding intended, my labors will not have been in vain.

J.D.R.

CHAPTER 1

Contextualization in Theology: A Discourse on Method

We have moved into a new period of theological reflection. The systems and system builders have done their work and passed from the scene. They left few if any heirs. There are many methods and diverse programs. David Tracy's *Blessed Rage for Order* symbolizes the fluid and transitional state of theology.

Some look at this situation and declare that the age of genius among theologians has passed. They lament the past and dread the future. But the fact that we are moving through a transitional period can also be met with challenge and anticipation. There are reasons why change must take place, but change—though eruptive—can be productive of qualitative improvement. I am daily impressed by the manner in which many of my contemporaries are meeting their theological task in view of changes in the situation to which they are called to respond. We shall first look at the traditional situation. Then we will assess the present climate in which the theologian is called to do his or her work, as a background for a description of the contextual method.

The Traditional Situation

Many of the pacesetters in theology did their work in the North Atlantic community, whether in French, German, or English. The theologians were all cousins, culturally speaking. The leadership was predominantly white and male. The theologians did their work in a climate in which there was a general presumption of the superiority of Western culture. Theology, no less than the churches, was part of a domesticated faith. Theologians were part of a "Constantinian captivity" of the faith.

The Greco-Roman classical tradition merged with the Judeo-Christian heritage to provide the intellectual and cultural milieu for theological discourse. Most of the theologians shared a similar racial or ethnic background. The context in which they did their theological work was in a sense homogeneous.

The philosophical perspectives of Plato and Aristotle, the Greek and Latin classics, and the entire mix of intellectual, moral, and scientific development in the West shape the theologians' theological thought.[1] The marriage between theology and culture was unquestioned during the patristic and medieval periods. Philosophy, either Platonic or Aristotelian, was the handmaiden of theology. It was only in the modern period that rational and scientific programs dethroned classical philosophy and questioned whether theology is queen of the sciences.

Many honest seekers after the truth were driven from the church. But fortunately many intellectual as well as spiritual giants remained in its ranks. They endeavored to render the faith respectable in spite of the attacks by "cultural despisers." Hume the skeptic is met by Kant the believer. Feuerbach and Nietzsche are matched by Schleiermacher, Kierkegaard, and Tillich. Even among theologians one finds a good balancing and self-correcting process. Karl Barth's special revelation is balanced by the general revelation of Emil Brunner and John Baillie. Jürgen Moltmann's political theology is in some sense a response to the strong existential posture of Rudolf Bultmann. What we observe, however, is mainly a family dialogue between white male Western theologians. If one adds American contributions, we do not get beyond the homogeneity of the cultural context of theologians of the North Atlantic community.

The New Situation

The new situation for theology is iconoclastic—it is not continuous. The climate is post-Barthian, cross-cultural, and interdisciplinary. Now enter liberation theologies, including feminine, black, and Hispanic programs. Theological development is vigorous throughout the southern hemisphere. This area represents two thirds of the human family and is described by Sergio Torres as those who live on the "underside of history." No longer is theology accepted as prepared and prepackaged and shipped by theologians of the North Atlantic theological community. The market for Western theology is diminishing as Third World theologians develop their own programs.

We live in a postcolonial world. Only rearguard resistance remains. There is no more time on the clock of history for colonialism. I agree with Leon Sullivan that the demise of apartheid is inevitable.

France is subjecting the peoples of several South Pacific islands to a state of oppression by using these islands to test nuclear weapons. We are polluting the environment and endangering the health of the living and the unborn. We have not dealt racism a mortal blow here at home in the United States. This is one important reason why our moral leadership in the world is so anemic.

These realities suggest that most nonwhite theology and feminist theology is done in the context of what José Miguez-Bonino calls "a revolutionary situation." The main rejoinder I hear from the theological establishment is that theology is universal. To assert that Western theology is universal is to fly in the face of compelling evidence. It is not universal. It takes a very provincial point of view and attempts to *totalize* it. The situation now demands that theology first be contextualized. This does not rule out the possibility of partnership in a pluralistic situation. If we reach a universal situation, it must take seriously the several contexts in which theological reflection is being done.

Those who want a secure and safe place to stand will find the present theological climate disturbing. The rise of strict evangelical and fundamentalist positions, together with witch-hunting and heresy trials, represents an attempt to cut off the more exploratory and fluid developments. There is always the danger that our faith may be severely tested by this new situation. There is also the possibility that some will move from one dogma to another. There is the risk that Christ might be uprooted in one context and set in concrete in another. Christ is above all cultures at the same time that he walks in and through them for their transformation and redemption. But we are forced into a situation of decision, and the future pulls us in a new direction.

Methodological Implications of Our New Situation

The mission of theology parallels somewhat the mission of the church. During the postcolonial age, the churches have had to make major concessions to the indigenizing process. Sending churches have had to enter into partnership with local Christians in order to be in any way effective. Missionaries have had to confront the rise of nationalism and the geopolitical realities of development and liberation. These realities have had a radical effect upon missiology and ministry.

In our own situation, we have a crisis situation. Racism, poverty, the feminization of poverty, and discrimination against women and homosexuals are grave concerns to be addressed. Unemployment and homelessness are rampant. The Government reports optimistic figures, but the real situations in which people live and suffer are getting worse. Affirmative action is being phased out with the national administration through the Department of Justice entering into litigation against constructive change. Farmers are going bankrupt by the thousands. Textile workers are being systematically dismissed as their work is being done by cheap labor abroad. The Civil Rights Commission, under the present leadership, is disgraceful and a waste of taxpayers' money. In my opinion, there is a direct relationship between the lack of leadership on moral issues at home and the soft policy related to apartheid in South Africa. In this crisis situation many theologians are concerned with the inerrancy of Scripture and the future rapture. Those who do get involved from the fundamentalist side seek to sanctify the political status quo.

We face in our midst the influx of large numbers of people from Third World countries. These people compete for jobs in a diminishing market. They are often willing to take menial jobs at low wages. This makes a bad situation worse. It pits the domestic poor against others coming in from the outside. We have not solved our race problem, and this additional mix of nonwhite peoples is taking place in a situation of jealousy and strife. We seem to think that the situation will heal itself without careful analysis and intervention on our part. But wishing will not make it so.

This multicultural and interethnic situation is explosive and it confronts us daily. The churches and seminaries seem to show a lack of sensitivity to what is going on outside their walls. They are preparing a ministry for an unreal world. There is no assurance that we will always minister to "our own kind." In the kind of world in which we live this expectation is both unrealistic and undesirable if we take the Great Commission seriously. Without a larger vision, the future of the Christian movement is dim.

For the most part, theology and theologians have been indifferent to these changes and new challenges. They have carried on with "business as usual" so far as theological reflection is concerned. Theological textbooks and theological courses of study and theological professors have generally continued to master the traditional material and pass the same on to their students. No exception is made for ethnic students or for Third World students who expect to minister in their home territories. The contextualization process proposed here should provide full exposure to the accumulated knowledge of the historic faith. But there should also be an encounter with the real world where witness is to take place, and a critical judgment should develop regarding text and context, so far as theological reflection is concerned.

Toward a Contextual Methodology

Theology needs to be developed in context. Paul Tillich's "answering" method is suggestive. Tillich desired to bring the historic faith into contact with the life situations of the believer. Theology and philosophy were to be partners in discussion. Philosophy would raise the questions and theology would provide the answers. Tillich's method of correlation has much insight that is useful. But his proposal as well as his program does not fully meet our present need. We would suggest that no philosophy, existential or otherwise, will be able to frame the questions that the present situation demands. The task is clearly interdisciplinary. To attempt to raise questions with any limited philosophical bias, such as process and Marxist, is inadequate. Context will help shape the questions as well as the theological response.

Theology in context may in fact lead to truly universal vision. John Cobb, I believe, has made some progress in this direction in his *Beyond Dialogue*. [2] Tillich also had attempted a conversation with Hindus and Buddhists,[3] but in my judgment Cobb's effort goes beyond Tillich to what he describes as "transformation." In pre-Barthian Protestantism, serious attempts at interreligious dialogue were made by Bishop Nathan Söderblom, William Temple, and Rudolf Otto. Howard Thurman, the black religious mystic poet and philosopher, deserves to be named in this company. Post-Vatican II Roman Catholic theology is worthy of mention.

We face a real danger even in our most creative projects of cross-cultural dialogue, theological or otherwise. We encounter a form of intellectual and spiritual neo-colonialism. The Western partners in the conversation usually do not "pass over" into another religion, culture, or theology as Cobb suggests. Rather, there is the tendency for Western partners to dominate. Latin American liberation theologians as well as some black and feminist theologians seem to follow Western theological scholarship in this regard. There is abundant evidence that the more "political" posture of liberation theology is the norm. The Ecumenical Association of Third World Theologians, made up of liberation theologians, is a case in point. Several volumes of the proceedings of these meetings have now been published. Thus one can examine the evidence.[4] Works by international evangelical and fundamentalist church persons and theologians are even less promising. The latter group is likely to add to status quo theology conservative political and economic perspectives that rule out humanization as a mandate of the gospel.

The time has come for all who participate in theological reflection —whether in Europe or the Americas, black, feminist, and Hispanic

—to allow theologians, especially in Africa and Asia, to do their own theological reflection. We need to leave them alone with their Bibles, with Christ, and with their own cultures and histories. There needs to be a moratorium on Western domination in the field of theology. We can learn much about liberation and compassion from the understanding of the gospel in the context of Asia and Africa. We do not seem prepared to listen, and neither do we accept their theologians as equal dialogue partners. Our theological reflection is poorer because of this.

Now let us look at how theological reflection should develop along contextual lines.

First, theology should be more interdisciplinary. In the past, systematic theology as well as dogmatics has been interdisciplinary in the internal sense. It has brought together such things as the Bible and the history of doctrine. But its interpretative instrument has generally been philosophy. Now it is necessary for theology to be interdisciplinary more in the external sense. For example, the social and natural sciences need to be taken seriously. Liberation theology, for example, draws heavily upon economics and political science. It is interesting that fundamentalism has entered the public arena without adequate attention to social analysis. There seems to be the assumption that inerrant Scripture provides the necessary answers.

What this new demand suggests is that theologians as individuals may no longer be able to master their subject field without cross-disciplinary teamwork. There will be a constant need to be in dialogue and collaboration across several disciplines in the humanities and in the social and natural sciences.

Second, the new situation will require that theology be ecumenical. Denominational affiliation will continue to be important, but there is need for ecumenical outreach in "faith and order" as well as in "life and work." One must occupy a theological position and work out of conviction. But the theologian will need to be in touch with the best literature on various doctrines of the faith. The source for truth transcends denomination as well as sex, race, and culture. No longer should one believe that only members of a particular race, nationality, sex, or culture can write a valid theology. At the present time, many of the best theological initiatives are coming from the southern hemisphere. The North Atlantic community no longer has a monopoly on theological reflection. Within a very short period, the Spanish language, once considered a barren theological language, has become a fruitful means to theological thought. We could illustrate this point as well through African and Asian theological developments. Neither should we gainsay the contribution of black, feminist, and other programs in the so-called First World. We stand in an ecumenical climate, even though we need an anchor in the historic faith.

Third, there is developing out of the pluralism of our day what Raimundo Panikkar has described as *ecumenical ecumenism.* Reference is made here to interreligious conversation. This dialogue must be North and South, not just East and West. We need to go beyond conversation with the so-called "great religions" and engage the primal religious traditions as well. The entire human family is within the range of our concern. Preliterate, prephilosophical, and nontextual religions are to be examined. This presents a methodological challenge to scholars who depend upon philosophy and textual criticism in theological discourse.

We can be specific about the need for cross-disciplinary exchanges regarding method and content in this endeavor. Theologians need to enter into conversation with historians of religions and cultural anthropologists as well as with biblical specialists and philosophers. There should be profound descriptive work prior to any subjective evaluation of religious phenomena. Again contextualization in history and culture is important to understanding. Examples would be conversations between Tillich and Mircea Eliade, between James Cone and John Mbiti, or between John Cobb and Mahayana Buddhists.

In this process, theologians have much to receive, but they also have much to give. As believers who confess a firm faith in a particular religious tradition, theologians have much to contribute to interreligious dialogue. Theologians can raise these discussions to an interconfessional level. This provides a depth of understanding that eludes pure objective study.

Fourth, it is refreshing to see the Bible pushed to the center of theological reflection. This is a great need. We see this trend in Roman Catholic theology in this post-Vatican II period. Protestant theology has emphasized the authority of Scripture from its inception. Yet this emphasis comes not only as a promise but as a threat to faith. Questions concerning the authority and proper interpretation of Scripture assume more urgency today. Theologians need careful exchanges with biblical scholars. But biblical scholars need the challenge of theological questions. Exegesis and hermeneutics need to be in constant tension. We need to know what the text meant, but we need also to understand what it means. We need to assess the authority of Scripture and seek to understand how it informs our life and community of faith in the context in which we stand. Our theological task must take biblical revelation and authority seriously.

Fifth, the historical perspective must not be sacrificed in the drive for relevance. We have made constant reference to the place of the historic faith as a point of reference. Our confessional tradition is more than this, it is an anchor for our faith. The theological task will continue to take historical research in the Christian movement seriously. As we deal with pluralism in our world, marked by the confluence of cultures, the perspective of history is an invaluable guide to what is the acceptable will of God in our context. Our historic confessions provide a place to stand as we examine the contemporary options and challenges to faith. In theological reflection as in life, hindsight is invaluable to foresight.

Sixth, closely related to the sense of history is the need for theological reflection to be rooted in the life and worship of the church, the believing community. Theology needs to be concerned about the church's mission and ministry. As an activity within the church, theology is at once priestly and prophetic. There needs to be a close relationship between theology and ministry, each having influence upon the other.

Seventh, theology should be political, but not partisan. In the contextualizing process we need to look at the concrete and particular situation. Theology should be sensitive to injustices and the violation of human rights. This should lead us into a concern for humanization beyond the Christian fellowship and outside the covenant of faith. We place the gospel in a situation of threat when we claim God's favoritism for us and distinguish between "we" and "they." If there is any sense in which we are chosen, it is for servanthood rather than favoritism. God *cares* for the oppressed, the poor (often the black and Hispanic in our midst), for women, children, and the aged, but God also has a salvific concern for oppressors, whoever they may be. Sometimes the oppressed are also oppressors. Theology has an ethical task. It must be concerned about liberation, humanization, and reconciliation.

Eighth, our theological reflection in context should seek holism. A relationship needs to be established between the secular and the sacred, body and soul, the cognitive, volitional, and affective aspects of the life of faith. The whole person and all of life should inform our theological task.

Ninth, theology must be particular but not provincial. We need to combine a concrete contextual orientation with a universal vision. Contextualization should lead to humanization for ourselves and the entire human family. The obvious weakness in much theology today is that it exalts God at the expense of human freedom and dignity. In fact, much oppression is sponsored in the name of God, whether Christian, Islamic, or Jewish. Religious intolerance is a root cause of much suffering today. Much suffering and death follow in the wake of Marxism which denies the existence of God. But many fundamental religionists also have bloody hands. It is not sufficient, therefore, to confess faith in God. God must also be understood as having an exalted character and a holy purpose for all creation, including human life.

Tenth, theology needs to be passionate without being irrational. Our epistemology needs to be carefully thought through. This is true of black theology as well as other theological programs. Theology needs intellectual integrity as well as religious fervor. As Afro-American theologians we can no longer denounce the intellectual task. We are entitled to explore other ways of thinking than that which is normative in the West, but we must *think.* Holistic thought is also thought, perhaps at a deeper level than cognition alone. Black theologians cannot escape the bicultural nature of their thinking. Our best thinking includes the best that we can derive from the Western tradition in theology, but more. Yet the reasons of the heart must be in tune with the reasons of the head. Faith must seek understanding.

We have begun to outline our vision of a contextual method in theological reflection. We have in mind an approach that is contextual in reach and in outreach. It is a means whereby the theologian seeks to know where he or she stands in a community of faith. But such an approach may also have ethnic and cultural traits. This inner understanding, identity, or commitment does not or should not lead to a self-righteous narrowness. It should lead instead to a profound cross-cultural and ecumenical encounter with those who stand outside the particular context of one's decision and life of faith. The goal is to get to know others in their context and in the depths of their commitment to the end that mutual understanding and enrichment may take place. It requires a greater grounding in faith to risk this encounter than it does to surround oneself with dogmatic structures of thought and faith. I believe that the way to spiritual growth and theological depth is by removing the walls of separation. It is not possible to build walls to keep others out without hemming oneself in. If one truly has a place to stand, confessionally, the way out is also the way in.

CHAPTER 2

African Roots
of Black Theology

The Afro-American's ancestry is African. The majority of blacks
came from what is now designated as West Africa. Because the
white Protestants sought to wipe out the essence of African traditional life, one has to look in Roman Catholic areas such as New
Orleans, the West Indies, or Brazil, in the New World for more
pronounced survivals of African culture. Black slaves were often
introduced to life in slavery in the Caribbean before they were
brought into the southern part of the United States. The Sea Islands off the coast of South Carolina and Georgia were sufficiently
isolated to retain some aspects of African language, religion, and
culture.

African Traditional Religion

J. Omosade Awolalu has contributed a valuable essay to our understanding of traditional African religion. We are told that this
indigenous religion has been handed down from generation to generation and is still alive and well. It is said to be a religion that
Africans today have made theirs by living and practicing it. It is a
religion that has no written literature, yet it is "written" everywhere
for those who care to see and read. Awolalu writes:

> It is largely written in the people's myths and folk tales, in their songs
> and dances, in their liturgies and shrines and in their proverbs and
> pithy sayings. It is a religion whose historical founder is neither known
> nor worshipped; it is a religion that has no zeal for membership drive,
> yet it offers persistent fascination for Africans, young and old.[1]

The outline of the fundamental beliefs of Africans by Awolalu is
worthy of repeating here. He sums up the credo of traditional African believers. They believe that:

(a) This world was brought into being by the Source of all beings known as the Supreme Being. This Supreme Being is given different names by different ethnic groups in Africa. These names are meaningful, and they reflect God's attributes and the people's concept of Him.

(b) The Supreme Being brought into being a number of divinities and spirits to act as His functionaries in the orderly maintenance of the world.

(c) Death does not write "the end" to human life, but the soul of the deceased who has lived well and "died a good death" will return to the Source of all beings and will continue to live in the abode of the departed spirits. Thus the ancestral cult is highly developed in Africa.

(d) The divinities and spirits together with the ancestral spirits are in a super-sensible world with the Supreme Being, but are not uninterested in what goes on in the world of men.

(e) The divinities and the ancestors have laid down some rules of conduct and guiding principles for the benefit of men and women and for the maintenance of peace and concord in the community.

(f) Man, the head of all creation, was created a moral agent, gifted with the ability to distinguish between right and wrong.

(g) When men observe the rules of conduct, they have the favor of the Supreme Being and His agents, and they enjoy *Shalom* (total well-being); when they act contrary, a breach occurs; sin is introduced. In other words, Africans hold that man is vitally related to and even dependent upon Deity and His agents who watch over human behavior and can reward or punish man as the case may be.[2]

Because of the geographical size and cultural diversity of black Africa, Kwame Gyekye is correct in confronting John Mbiti for his generalizations about African tribal religions.[3] The main burden of Gyekye's critique of Mbiti is his concept of time as two-dimensional, past and present. Mbiti's failure to recognize an awareness of the future is critical. It leaves a convenient gap in the African perspective for Mbiti to embrace the Western belief in progress and proclaim the Christian doctrine of last things. While Gyekye recognizes similarities among religions in Africa, he is sure from his direct experience and knowledge of the Akan that they hold a three-dimensional conception of time. He knows this from his study of the Akan language and proverbs as well as the activities of diviners and medicine men in communities.

Mbiti draws certain unfortunate conclusions for all of Africa from his "tissue of errors" based upon his so-called African concept of time. Not only does he make a case for Christian eschatology by the lack he views in the African concept of time but he also draws social and political conclusions from it. Mbiti feels that the defective concept of time accounts for political, economic, and ecclesiastical instability in Africa.[4]

Another problem Gyekye unearths has to do with Mbiti's view on African ethical philosophy. Mbiti asserts that Africans do not consider something evil because of its "intrinsic nature" but because of its results. They are concerned with the rank or status of a person harmed by an evil action. While a person of lower rank might be held responsible for doing harm to someone of higher rank, someone of higher rank would not be held responsible for an offense against someone of lower rank. Since older people hold more rank over younger people in traditional African societies, one might argue that it is in order for an elderly person to take property from a younger person. This would imply that African communities have no objective moral rules. Again, Gyekye argues that this is not the case with Akan society. Evil is seen as reprehensible, irrespective of the doer—it is intrinsic in nature. Gyekye writes (*Second Order*, p. 93):

> There is a species of evil referred to by Akans as *musuo*. This is considered to be a great evil which affects the whole community and brings shame upon it. . . . *Musuo* . . . is thus universally reprehensible by virtue of its *intrinsic nature.*

Awolalu's essay on "sin" in traditional African religion would uphold Gyekye's criticism of Mbiti on the moral issue.[5] This broadens the base for the exception to Mbiti's hasty conclusion, since Awolalu represents the Yoruba tradition.

It is significant that other African scholars are beginning to question seriously the generalizations and hasty conclusions of Mbiti. He is to be lauded for his attempt to identify with the traditional African cultures of East Africa. But he seems to interpret what he finds mainly from the perspective of ready-made theological premises. He sees a direct relationship between black theology and southern Africa. This he views mainly in political terms. He pokes fun at the Negritude movement in Francophone Africa which grew out of a dialogue between black and African literati in Paris. While most African theologians are excited about the dialogue with black colleagues of the African Diaspora, Mbiti has kept a safe distance. It is high time, therefore, that African scholars should seriously challenge Mbiti's influence, especially in the West. It is characteristic for Western theologians to "use" a representative speaker against the liberation of the oppressed. It is in order, therefore, that certified African religious and philosophical spokespersons, other than Mbiti, now make their day in court.

One cannot claim absolute continuity between African traditional religion and black religious experience. To do so would be to fly in the face of an abundance of contrary evidence. Too much time and too many circumstances divide Africans from Afro-Americans. The divergence between E. Franklin Frazier and Melville Herskovits as to the extent to which Africanisms have survived slavery among blacks in the United States has been much discussed. The slave system broke down the linguistic and cultural patterns of the Africans. Yet the influence of African music, rhythm, and dance is unmistakable in black culture. It is quite obvious that slaves did not come to America without any religious traditions. In a word, since Africa is a historic reality for blacks, the African background to the understanding of black religious experience will always be important. Any enlightenment we can bring through studies made by Africans themselves is needed.

The Place of the Bible

A serious theological project requires careful biblical study. I have been deeply impressed by the importance given to Scripture by German theologians such as Gerhard von Rad and Ernst Käsemann. Theologians looked to them as their mentors along with Karl Barth and Frederich Schleiermacher. History of doctrine or philosophical schools did not eclipse the place of the Bible.

One might almost contrast this with the deemphasis upon the Bible among process theologians who have pushed the Bible into the background and shoved the metaphysics of Alfred North Whitehead into the foreground. On the other hand, there are examples where Bible study clearly overshadows theology. Southern Baptist Theological Seminary at Louisville represents an example of the latter. Without being judgmental about programs in these cases, I am suggesting that it would be beneficial for Bible and theology to inform each other.

In this regard black theology has a special role to play. The black experience of the Christian faith has centered in the Bible. As we study African traditional religions, we understand why black slaves embraced the Bible spontaneously.

Aylward Shorter writes about the "content" of African traditional religions. We mention his brief summary here because it enlarges our understanding of the black slave's response to Scripture. Shorter outlines five characteristics of African religious experience: (1) The vision of wholeness or integration of life—"sacred" and "profane" are relative terms. (2) Conscious symbolism as a means of communication. Through symbols, Africans bridge the sacred and the secular; it is through symbols that the sacred is spoken of in secular terms; symbols make an integrated and balanced view of reality possible. (3) Affirmation of the "fecundity" of life, which refers to a great value placed upon physical generation, upon life and the sharing of life. Great stress is placed upon interpersonal relationships and the value of the human person. (4) Related to fecundity, the emphasis placed upon "man-in-community"—for example, by Léopold Senghor, Julius Nyerere, and Kenneth Kaunda. This includes the nature of the community, the freedom of the individual within the community, and the responsibility of the individual for the community. (5) The relationships between human and spiritual beings, for example, between the living and the dead.[6]

Shorter does not mention the concept of God. The belief in a Supreme Being, with similar attributes, is almost universal in black Africa, apart from the influence of Islam or Christianity. In spite of the writings of European and American scholars, African theologians do not hesitate to assert that the traditional understanding of God is similar in nature and attributes to the God of the Bible. This is especially true of creation and providence as activities of the Supreme Being. The traditional African conception of God is also monotheistic. The lesser spirits are God's ministers in relation to human beings. In many ways this God resembles most the God of the Old Testament.

When African slaves were introduced to the Bible, they were able to derive meanings from it that were hidden to the oppressors. They understood God against the background of traditional beliefs in a Supreme Being. They were aware of both the power and the moral uprightness of God. Jehovah, as described in the Old Testament, was a close facsimile of the African Supreme Being they had known. As they faced a situation of great hardship, the liberation of the Hebrews from Egyptian bondage caught their fancy. For the black oppressed, facing daily the white oppressors, the exodus took on a political as well as a religious meaning. They believed that something would happen in heaven and on earth when they sang, "Go down, Moses, 'way down in Egypt land;/Tell ole Pharaoh, Let my people go!"

Because of their understanding of life as sacred, life as whole, life as community, the slaves were drawn to the Bible. But their understanding of the Bible differed from that of the slave masters. The beliefs the slaves brought with them and the oppressed conditions under which they lived were two important reasons for this difference.

An increasing number of black scholars are specializing in the Bible. But some are hesitant to commit themselves in print and others refuse to take up the challenge that black theology presents. The Bible is so central for the black experience that a "blackenization" of biblical exegesis would be the most rewarding and important contribution they could possibly make in a lifetime. My own attempts to reread the Bible in the light of black religious experience has opened up truths from those sacred texts I have not found in the most learned Western biblical scholars. Exegesis from below, seen in solidarity with the oppressed, yields insights missed by those who read the Bible in solidarity with the privileged.

The work being done by Christian Marxist scholars in Europe opens a new window, but it is one-sided. The Bible is personal-spiritual as well as social-political. It is at once priestly and prophetic. To contrast one aspect of religious experience with the other is to miss the holistic biblical message. José Miranda, a Latin American biblical exegete, helps us to understand the biblical grounding for social justice in *Marx and the Bible*. John Bennett is probably correct when he observes that the title "may keep the scholars who need to read it most from reading it." He expresses, however, deep appreciation for the content of this work: "It massively presents the case for the identification of God with the cause of transforming justice that for the most part the church has resisted or from which the church has diverted Christians to privatistic or bland forms of religion."[7]

The Marxist entrée into biblical exegeses leaves much to be desired. While it contributes much to an interpretation of Scripture by relating the gospel of liberation to economic, social, and political injustices in our group life, it does not handle with equal facility the spiritual dimensions of our personal existence.

The most balanced view of biblical interpretation seems to flow from the understanding of black scholars and preachers. One gets a feel for the holistic message of the Bible in the sermons of Martin Luther King, Jr., and the meditations of Howard Thurman which speak to the whole person and all of life.

Among black theologians, James Cone has treated scriptural interpretation more completely than anyone else. But since his hermeneutical perspective is Western (either/or), perhaps Teutonic, he operates in a one-sided manner. No committed black church leader or scholar would wish to tone down his liberation motif. Our people have endured and are enduring too much deep ethnic suffering for that. But the oppression-liberation formula does not adequately unlock the biblical message.

Robert Bennett and Charles Copher are among black Old Testament scholars who have begun serious study, relating their knowledge of Old Testament sources to the black religious experience. Both writers have considered Africa in the biblical period.[8] Bennett has done some work with black theologians in view. His writings have been well researched; they are critical and informative.

Thomas Hoyt has examined the influence of the poverty message of the Old Testament upon King's exegesis. Hoyt writes:

> Although the love principle as encompassed by the life and teachings of Jesus informed Dr. King, it was the Old Testament which played a central role in his political exegesis. This is proper in that Israel assumed the vocation of living out God's demands for national and political life.[9]

Hoyt reminds us that there is no presuppositionless exegesis. King, he reports, came to black people and brought a message of hope to the poor and the oppressed in the language they knew well.

> There was hardly a black man or woman who was not familiar with the language of the biblical narrative, and so when he drew on the story of Moses and the Exodus, all black folk knew precisely what he was talking about. They were familiar with the account of how God had delivered his people out of their bondage. Moreover, there was close parallel to the living conditions of the two peoples, separated by such great distances in time. Both peoples were being held in bondage in a strange land; both peoples were treated harshly by their masters as being poor because of their laziness; both peoples felt a close affinity with Yahweh as their defender and protector, and both saw a relationship between poverty and piety. In fact, the whole Biblical drama could be told in terms of the relationship between God and a poor, oppressed people.[10]

Hoyt insists that the exegetical approach adopted at any particular period will be closely connected on the one hand to the estimation held of the Scriptures as a whole and on the other hand to the entire social context. King therefore saw the Scriptures as providing archetypical experiences that were conducive to understanding the times. His method was to retell the story that would force the oppressors to hear again the sound of freedom and cause the oppressed to experience hope and motivation for the pursuance of freedom. This was political exegesis which helped pave the way for black theology. Hoyt concludes that King helped us understand that God identifies with and empowers the powerless and that the Bible is relevant to political theory and practice.

Hoyt has made an important contribution to our understanding of King's use of Scripture, especially the Old Testament. King's understanding of the entire Bible is essential to complete the picture. Without a consideration of King's understanding of the love ethic of Jesus, one does not have a complete understanding of his exegetical program. It is clear that King had a message of reconciliation as well as liberation from his reading of Scripture. He believed in the unity of the Bible. For him the God of Amos was also the God of Jesus. And, finally, King had a holistic understanding of persons. Since the New Testament has been privatized, futurized, and eschatologized by Western scholars, the black perspective on the New Testament may save this part of the Scripture and in so doing save the church from spiritual and moral bankruptcy. The Bible has an important place in black theology.

Conclusion

This brief chapter describes the Afro-American religious and theological heritage against the background of traditional African religions. The assumption is that contemporary African scholarship is essential for a more profound understanding of African religious experience than was previously available.

Assuming that there is continuity as well as discontinuity between Africa past and present and Afro-American experience, we have identified some fundamental insights into the development of black theology out of the African background. The Bible is an important document for the black church and the development of black theology. Thus we have indicated why the Bible made so much sense to black slaves when they were first introduced to it. Finally, we illustrate how the Bible has received some fresh and powerful interpretations by key black theologians, mainly biblical theologians.

CHAPTER 3

An Afro-American/African
Theological Dialogue

One of the most difficult assignments for a Christian theologian who has interest in worldwide religious phenomena is to find a framework for discussion. Yet in this time of world history, when all human beings live in a global village, the task is inescapable. The confluence of cultures, the provisions of science and technology, and many other factors compel us to enter into dialogue with currents of religious life, experience, and thought from all peoples. It is appropriate that those of us with roots in Third World cultures should consider this task an urgent and serious one.

This reaching out in interreligious dialogue is easier for those with nonconfessional approaches. Scholars in philosophy, anthropology, and the history of religions, for instance, can join in two-way conversation with less effort than theologians who interpret the faith of a believing community with absolute claims. The Western bias of these other disciplines may be an impediment, but it does not completely rule out the potential for dialogue. But theology by its own self-understanding in the Western tradition finds little ground for even a possibility for conversation outside that tradition. Add to this problem the excess baggage of the civilization that has developed in the North Atlantic world and one gets some appreciation of the difficulties involved.

The case for Catholics differs from that of Protestants, though both have problems with this task. Protestants are often hampered by an exclusive Christocentric revelation; while Catholics have held to a belief that there is no salvation outside the church. Of course, there are Protestants who hold a more inclusive view of Christology. Likewise, many Catholics, since Vatican II, have a more open ecclesiology. But the alienation from Third World cultures and religions is almost a constant factor. The shadow and often the reality of colonialism and racism stand as barriers to real dialogue. The present discussion is limited to the Protestant experience in these matters.

The Contextual Bias of Western Theology and Third World Response

Western explorations into the religious history of humankind have been informed by a colonial mentality. This perspective has influenced the selection of the materials of religion and culture to be examined. Only those characteristics in the thought and experience of non-Westerners which have a similarity to Western civilization have received consideration. The fact is that a superiority complex dominates the scene. This has been reinforced by the evolutionary élan that has been operative in the quest for origins in the history of religions. Religions and cultures have been classified by the schema established by the evaluation of the materials set up by the West.

Philologists, philosophers, and anthropologists, often associated with the British colonial administration in India, for example, discovered Sanskrit and profound schools of philosophy, which made them aware of a whole new universe of thought and religious experience. This discovery of Sanskrit, a language hewed to logical and mathematical perfection, made the science of language a possibility. Furthermore, the profound thought and mystic expression of the sages of India must have been a profound blow to the egos of the first Western investigators. It is fortunate that the approach of these nonconfessional scholars was more affirmative than that of the Christian theologians and missionaries who invaded these lands. A real dialogue did take place in which the intellectual and spiritual riches of the East flowed into Western minds and hearts.

Christian missionaries armed with the gospel and informed by the exclusive claims of theologians ignored these religions and philosophies as much as possible. When this proved impossible they branded what they found as "heathen." At best they described what they found in non-Western cultures as only a preparation for the gospel. The missionaries carried with them the pride of race and culture and cooperated with the colonial administrators (as some American missionaries have recently aided the CIA) in raping these peoples of their resources and their very humanity. They were confident that God had smiled upon the West and that God would give them victory and an abundant harvest as the Christian colonizers of the non-Western world.

Christians affirm God's providence. This implies that God runs history. We should not be surprised, therefore, to observe that God's intentions for non-Westerners varied from that of many Christian missionaries. *The Christian Century,* a popular church journal in the United States, was given its name because there was the assumption that during the twentieth century all human beings would be claimed for Christ. Most of those who founded that publication did not live to see the last quarter of this century. We now observe that they did not foresee the impact that the social, economic, and political revolutions would have upon their prediction. In the Third World where Christian missionaries expected such an abundant harvest, Marxism and nationalism, informed by an awakening of traditional cultural consciousness, have radicalized the situation beyond any vision available at the turn of this century.

At the very time that Westerners had begun to adjust to the social and cultural revolution in Asia, Africa arose as a slumbering giant and presented its credentials upon the stage of world history. This is most disturbing because it has been assumed that before Europeans went to Africa for the purpose of colonizing it, only the worst form of barbarism existed there. So effective was this propaganda that many blacks and whites assumed that slavery was a great improvement over the African situation. It was believed that in the providence of God slavery had been established both to Christianize and to civilize blacks from Africa.

African traditional religions had been dismissed as mere magic or superstition. It was assumed that sub-Sahara Africa (Black Africa) was totally uncivilized. But serious scholarship by historians and anthropologists from within and without Africa compels us to take a second look. The evidence is overwhelming that we had found there what we looked for and did not tap the riches of the cultures already there.

We thus are confronted by a bold and open challenge to those aspects of Western scholarship, especially that of Christian theologians and church leaders, which have made our approach to the Third World mainly a monologue. We have attempted to prepackage theology in our cultural containers and transport and impose these upon the minds and hearts of non-Westerners. In our eyes their only response could be to appropriate our ready-made gospel to their situation. This required of them a passive mentality and a low level of cultural consciousness.

The fact that the conditions for blind acceptance of our theologies are passing has now dawned upon many. History itself and secular events, more than anything else, may force us to realize that the golden age for Western theology and missionary activity has passed into history. What Soki Coe, an Asian theologian, describes as the "contextualization" of theology is the order of the day in Asia, Africa, Latin America, and the islands of the seas. There is a creative and aggressive mining of traditional cultures and religions for perspectives that will make the gospel speak with relevance of salvific power in the hearts and lives of peoples everywhere. Because the earthly condition of many of these peoples is riddled with poverty, racism, classism, and rampant misery, the gospel is being understood as God's word of deliverance *in time* as well as *in eternity.*

The Theological Impasse

Karl Barth's *Nein* to Brunner concerning natural revelation is symbolic of the theological impasse I wish now to describe. It may be possible to find somewhere in Barth's extensive writings that he changed his mind or that he really did not mean what he said. The fact remains that fruitful discussion with non-Western religious traditions was going on before Barth but that the overawing impact of his distinction between Christianity and other religions eclipsed the important work of Nathan Söderblom, Rudolf Otto, and others in this important field.

Otto's *Idea of the Holy,* Heiller's *Prayer,* Söderblom's *Living God,* Temple's *Nature, Man and God,* and similar studies in Holland had opened up a deep appreciation by Protestant theologians for the possibility of a two-way conversation between Christians and religionists of other traditions. Some of these studies are useful only in dealing with religions with a sacred book, advanced belief systems, and exalted philosophical concepts. The phenomenological studies, however, move into a comparison of any and all belief systems.

For almost a half century this significant theological tradition among Protestant theologians has been in a state of hibernation. Only a few mute attempts have been made to reestablish the august tradition of the pre-Barthian period. Notwithstanding the arguments by pro-Barthians that Barth was not responsible for this state of affairs, the continual reign of Barth through his disciples and the absence of chairs in comparative religions in West German universities provide much plausibility for the conclusions I have drawn.

The most significant studies have been made by historians of religions and philosophers such as Mircea Eliade, Cantwell Smith, William Ernest Hocking, and S. Radhakrishnan, to name only a few. These interpreters of religious experience are more appropriately classified as phenomenologists of religion than as theologians. It is worth mentioning that some theologians, such as Paul Tillich, Nels Ferré, John Cobb, and John Hick, have become greatly concerned about reviving the earlier conversation with religionists of other faiths. But it has been mainly nontheological interpreters of religious experience who have kept the tradition of Otto and Söderblom alive. They provide a vital link from that stage to the present.

The circumstances of human history, especially the cry for liberation by the wretched of the earth, are going to force Western theologians to overcome the Barthian formula in regard to the scope of God's revelation in creation, history, and the cultures of peoples everywhere. Barth's attitude toward non-Christian religions was championed by Hendrik Kraemer, a Dutch missiologist and theologian, during the 1940s and 1950s. While we are not advocating a syncretism among religions; we are, however, asserting that the exclusive Christology that is prepackaged in the cultures of the North Atlantic theological community must now become inclusive so that the God who is in Christ as "Emmanuel" can be known and confessed as "Lord of all."

Black/African Theologies: A Look at the Task

There can hardly be a better example in which to contextualize what has gone before than the black/African theological situation. *Black* here refers to the Afro-American. *African* refers to the peoples of Africa mainly south of the Sahara Desert. In pursuing the subject, we are aware of continuity and discontinuity between blacks and Africans. After Alex Haley's *Roots* it is to be assumed that most people are open to the possibility that the African influence upon blacks is a reality. The African ancestry for blacks is taken for granted here. The consciousness of this in recent years has created a cultural dialogue with all peoples of African descent, including those in the West Indies and South America. This dialogue has reached a more intense form between blacks in the United States and African countries than it has elsewhere. As a participant in this transatlantic dialogue, I will limit the present discussion to this phase.

While West, Central, and East African countries are generally postcolonial, vestiges of colonialism and rampant racism abide in southern Africa. Against this background the dialogue with Africans in the extreme south is restricted. It can usually take place only when Africans from the south can meet in other African countries or abroad. But the impact of the mutual exchange between African theologians and church leaders from South Africa and black theologians is immediate and powerful because of their common experience of racism. Both know racism as their archenemy. The encounter of the Christian faith with racism in both cases puts a dynamic content into the meaning of black consciousness and power for a deeper understanding of the gospel. The dialogue is highly sociopolitical and has an accusing word of judgment for white oppressors in both situations. Liberation from the reality of institutionalized racism takes priority in this discussion.

The encounter between blacks and Africans in independent nations is more intense at the point of contextualizing the faith in the cultures of Africa. Here the common experience of overcoming the scars of the past oppression can be shared. The mind and spirit of blacks and Africans alike must be decolonized. Black consciousness as developed in black theology can be a useful model in developing a sense of pride and self-determination in both settings.

There is a common temperament in African independent churches and black cults and sects in the inner cities of the United States. The common source is African traditional religions and cultures. Thus historical and phenomenological studies in these tribal religions will cast significant light upon our shared investigations.

What is clear is that theological programs, however Christological, that are made in Western countries are methodologically and contextually inadequate to interpret the gospel in these new situations. The old wineskins made in theological centers in Europe and America will not contain the new wine. As a citizen in the First World with an ancestry in the Third World, I cannot but take this theological challenge with all seriousness. Indeed, it becomes increasingly difficult for anyone anywhere to think narrowly and draw a circle that leaves out two thirds of the human race. In our global village, a theological circle with such a limited circumference cannot be tolerated any more than a political one.

African/Black Theology: The Quest

Edward W. Fasholé-Luke helps to clarify the issue when he writes on "The Quest for African Christian Theologies."[1] He qualifies his subject by the adjective "Christian" and the plural "theologies." He therefore makes it clear that he is not writing a general African cultural theology based on traditional belief systems. Furthermore, he makes it clear that there can be no single monolithic program for a Christian African theology. As a black theologian, I would agree with this outlook and assert the same regarding black theologies and also the need to specify the "Christian" content of our programs. The reasons for this agreement may differ, but the description of what is going on in Africa and Afro-America is accurate. It is unfair to the creativity and rich varieties in theological expression in either case to single out one black or African theologian as *the theologian.* African theologians remind us that Mbiti is not the only African theologian. In Germany, it has been often necessary for me to say that James Cone is not the only black theologian. No one theologian should carry this burden. If weaknesses are found in one program, the entire enterprise is then suspect. It would be unfortunate to write off either African or black theology without a serious examination of an increasing number of able theologians on both continents.

Fasholé-Luke's use of the word "quest" also indicates a profound insight. A few years ago Fr. Gardiner and I released a collection of essays similarly entitled *Quest for a Black Theology*.[2] What is being implied by "quest" in both cases is the stage of progress of these theological programs. Black theology in the United States may be more developed than African Christian theology, but it is not yet beyond the "questing" stage. It will take the serious teamwork of many specialists for several years to complete a task so great and so nobly begun.

There are other African theologians who support the main outlook of Fasholé-Luke. For instance, Kwesi Dickson writes from Ghana and J. W. Zvomunonita Kurewa from Rhodesia concerning the development and the meaning of a *Theologia Africana*.[3] What we are saying is that both African and black theologies are relatively new. However, neither is in its infancy and both have now reached a serious level of development.

These theological movements, on two continents, present a serious challenge to Western theology. They have a significant contribution to make to both theology and the church around the world. These theologies are now ready and anxious for dialogue. But they will insist upon their contextual validity and integrity of thought. They will not participate in a one-way conversation.

Method and Authority in Black/African Theologies

We are now prepared to take a brief look at thought patterns and sources of authority in black/African theologies. In this section we will reflect upon epistemology, Scripture, and tradition.

Epistemology

The problem of knowledge is acute for theology because of the confessional aspect of the subject matter. While theologians deal with many of the same problems and concepts as do philosophers, they also work within the context of a confession of faith and belief in divine revelation. This is precisely the reason why a theory of knowledge presents such a serious challenge to the theologian.

Karl Barth identified the problem of epistemology as one of the primary factors in his dispute with Schleiermacher. Barth saw

Schleiermacher as reasoning from the human to the divine. Barth, on the contrary, insisted that revelation comes from God to the human. How we treat the knowledge question in theology is foundational to everything else.

My own development has been varied. It includes Christian Platonism, neo-orthodoxy, British neo-liberalism, American liberation theology, and the theology of the social gospel. Ethics and phenomenology of religion are very influential in my outlook. Cone has been greatly influenced by Barth, French existentialism, and Tillich, to mention some currents in his thought. The black experience is fundamental in understanding either of us. African theologians are often influenced by Western sources, but the African personality radiates throughout their thought.

The issue being raised, however, is whether fresh ways of thinking are emerging out of the "African presence" in African and black theologies. For instance, black consciousness has caused Afro-American theologians to mine the rich spiritual heritage of their history for the language of faith. African poets and philosophers have developed the concept of negritude. Furthermore, we are exploiting the use of metaphors, parables, folktales, and stories for a forceful language within which to interpret the gospel. The common language and mode of thought among peoples of African descent is existential—but also communal. It is therefore holistic. Thought includes feeling and participation. Basil Matthews, of Trinidad, refers to black thought as *soulful, lived* thought.

Professor Hajime Nakamura of Tokyo University wrote a classic book entitled *The Ways of Thinking of Eastern Peoples.* He treated thought patterns in Japan, China, Tibet, and India. A companion volume might describe the manner of thought among African peoples. In both cases, we are dealing with a tradition in thought that is not identical with the either/or perspective of the West. Readings in the writings of such nontheological thinkers as Kenneth Kaunda, Léopold Senghor, and Julius Nyerere illustrate this point.

Just as Asian scholars are searching the classics of the Orient to find contextual ways of doing theology, even so African and Afro-American scholars are creatively at work in their own intellectual and cultural traditions. Theology can no longer be prepared in Europe or America and merely transplanted to the Third World. The Platonic/Aristotelian tradition that has guided theological reflection for two thousand years is being challenged head on. Black theologians with ancestry in Africa are participating creatively in this dialogue. It is unfortunate that most Western scholars seem totally unaware that any of this is going on.

The Place of the Bible

Biblical interpretation is extremely important in both black and African theologies. One of the first important team efforts of African theologians was to produce the book entitled *Biblical Revelation and African Beliefs.* [4] Among important treatments of the subject in Black America, one should note James Cone's essay "Biblical Revelation and Social Existence,"[5] Robert Bennett's "Black Experience and the Bible,"[6] and Thomas Hoyt's "The Biblical Tradition of the Poor and Martin Luther King, Jr."[7] Furthermore, major works by several black and African scholars place special emphasis upon the Bible as the textbook for "black belief."

The Bible, for blacks, is a "living book." Recognition of the creative and providential involvement of God in the history of the people of the Old Testament is basic to black interpretation. A direct relationship through faith exists between God's acts of liberating Israel and the freedom struggle of blacks. In black theology there is no "quest" for the historical Jesus. Jesus is present as a Divine Friend. The prophets speak for God in judgment against the dehumanization of the poor and the weak. But there is also an awareness of sin and guilt and the need for forgiveness among blacks. Black theology also recognizes God's forgiveness of the oppressor who meets God's demands for justice and love toward the needy and the helpless. This is not "cheap grace," for it includes the acceptance of the dignity and equality of all human beings and the sharing of power.

We now understand, through our conversation with Africans, why black slaves never accepted the version of the Bible that white slavery preachers and theologians gave them. By instinct they knew that the God of the Bible hated slavery. The traditional religions of Africa have much in common with the faith and ethics of the Bible. Therefore, without theological education, indeed without exposure to education at all, black slaves understood God to be just and loving. Because of their suffering, black people have always seen the Bible as a Book of Consolation. But because of their understanding of God, they have also recognized the Bible as a prophetic book. It has been, and still is, for blacks an incendiary document against injustices, but at the same time it speaks of the salvific assurance of forgiveness for each sinner before God.

There is therefore a longing among both black and African systematic theologians for a supportive cadre of able biblical scholars from among their ranks. Prospects for the growth of such a group of biblical scholars with the needed sensitivity are not too encouraging. Some are not touched by black consciousness and still repeat uncritically their Euro-American sources. Others are lured away from this mandate by attractive offers that take them out of the movement. Consequently, theologians are forced to do their own exegesis and develop their own hermeneutics and get on with the business at hand. After all, this appears to be exactly what theological pacesetters like Barth and Tillich did and perhaps for similar reasons.

Tradition

Any Christian theology worthy of the name must take the Christian tradition seriously. Black and African theologies tend to do this. There appear, however, to be two traditions throughout most of the church's history so far as the social consciousness of the church is concerned. These are the *conservative* tradition and the *radical* tradition. Just recently I visited the city of Constance on the German-Swiss border. It was here that John Hus was condemned by a church council and burned. This is a shocking reminder of the tension between reactionary and radical factions in church history. Black and African theologians continue to take the history of the Christian movement seriously, but they maintain a critical distance. They find much that they can accept, much that they must reject, and much that they must reinterpret.

Ellewaha E. Mshana gives an account of two conferences between black and African church leaders and theologians in East Africa. The agreement of these two assemblies at Dar es Salaam, Tanzania (1971), and at Kampala, Uganda (1972), was to the effect that black theology and African theology are programs of contextualization and liberation though the situations are not identical. Because there are differences, Africans must speak for themselves. Mshana quotes from George Thomas, an Afro-American professor of theology, who described black theology as "a religious description, interpretation and expression of the life style and God consciousness of black people, beginning in the African experience into the black diaspora."[8] In sum, Thomas is asserting that black theology comes out of the black church which comes out of black religion having its roots in the African experience.

Mshana, who teaches at the Lutheran Theological College, Makumira, Tanzania, and who edits the *Africa Theological Journal,* observes (p. 21):

> To hear the African Theology we have to go and listen to the African preachers, laymen, catechists, teachers and ordinary believers in Christ and hear what the Gospel means to them. . . . We have to look

for ways in which the Christian faith is being implanted in African art
forms, music, drama, traditional . . . dances, stories, proverbs, wise
sayings, analogies, metaphors. . . . We have to go to our African
Traditional religion. . . . We have to translate the Christian truth into
African thought forms . . . language . . . terminologies.

What is needed is that the church and theology be decolonized.
The apologetic needs of African Christians must be couched in
African ways of thinking. "Just as Greeks Hellenized Christianity
and Europeans Europeanized Christianity Africans must now Afri-
canize Christianity" (p. 26). And thus there is a unity in diversity in
the contextualization of black and African theologies. But the reading of tradition is remarkably similar. Neither blacks nor Africans
are at home with the tradition of ecclesiology or theology imposed
upon them by Euro-American traditions (p. 28).

Some Cardinal Christian Doctrines

Jacob Neusner, of Brown University, has asserted that contemporary Jewish theology finds its context in the Holocaust.[9] In like
manner I see the negative influences giving rise to African and black
theology as colonialism and racism—either or both. The positive
sources are the rich cultural and spiritual traditions in Africa that
persist in the religious and cultural aspects of Afro-American life.
It is this mix which provides the setting for a reconception of Christian theology.

Theism

Africans and blacks live in a pool of divinity. The fundamental
question has not to do with the existence of God, for there are gods
many and lords many. The God question is centered around the
nature and character of God. We are often in need of a deeper
understanding regarding creation and providence. We are equally
in need of an insight into God's redemptive plan. But an approach
to God that considers only personal salvation at some future time
does not meet the demands of faith for a suffering people.

Oppression that leads to ethnic suffering casts the God question
in a different context. One has to search for the meaning of life and
historical existence while facing the negativities of life. We must ask
often if God cares. Does God really bear our griefs and carry our
sorrows? The questions Why? and How long? are often on the
hearts and minds of blacks. In a world in which racism is rampant
and where, as Cone says, "to be Black is to be blue," the question

of identity, both personal and ethnic, looms large. The issue is not really whether God is the same complexion or hue as we. The color of God is ancillary to the prior question regarding God's character. We earnestly desire to know whether God cares. Thus questions regarding the creation, passivity, and the providence of God move with the drift of our concern for the saving purpose of God. The nature of God talk or the shape of theism will reflect the circumstances of the existential and ethnic peculiarity of Africans and blacks. Furthermore, the cultural consciousness of Africans and blacks, together with the identity crises triggered by racism or colonialism, forms the context for the formulation of the theistic hypothesis in black/African theologies.

When pressed to do more for the minorities in the United States, President Carter responded that "life is not fair." Blacks and Africans have lived in this climate in which life is "unfair." What understanding of the Divine will enable us to make sense out of the unfairness of life? What view of God will give us the courage to seek changes in a system that has humiliated us and robbed us of our God-given dignity? No statement on God that does not emerge out of our cultural history or that does not take sides regarding oppression and liberation will be meaningful to the oppressed today. Thus theistic interpretations coming ready-made from Marburg, Oxford, or Harvard may be edifying to the mind but not to the hearts and lives of the blacks and Africans who are still among Frantz Fanon's "wretched of the earth." The task of black theology is to take what can be salvaged from theologians in the North Atlantic communities and translate this into the idiom of those oppressed millions who need a liberating understanding of God that is politically and not merely spiritually oriented.

We need a God who is Being, *not* Becoming. We need a God who suffers *for* and *with* the weak and the helpless. We need a God whose power is matched by a will for good. We need a God whose love is undergirded by justice. We need a God who reveals a saving purpose *in* history, not merely *above* and *beyond* history. The biblical God is, for us, One whose holy purpose for human life is manifest not just in salvation history but through all creation, in world history and among all peoples.[10]

Community

Africans are saying that "communion of saints" must include reverence for ancestors. The formula "Because I am we are" is a powerful affirmation in Africa. The sense of family extends not only in space but in time. It reaches outward in terms of kinship to the living, and moves backward in time as well. Thus there is a communion between the "living" and the "living dead."

Among Afro-Americans the family system based on blood ties has been severely assaulted by oppression (slavery, discrimination, racism), and new forms of togetherness have moved in to fill the void. Kinship ties of a nonblood type forged out of the necessity for survival have developed in the most unlikely places. Large families often adopt more children on an informal basis. Because of shortages in housing and the high cost of housing, many people from small towns move into the same house or apartment. In a hostile urban setting they pool their resources and develop a sense of belonging as a surrogate family. And most of all, our black churches take on the character of a large extended family.

It is not surprising that the concept of *ujamaa* from Swahili has been adopted by blacks as a way of expressing this new sense of peoplehood. Black churches therefore are seeking an in-depth understanding of their group life as "familyhood." This experience has significance for our theological statement on the black church. The nature and mission of the church as an extended family made up of believers in Christ is the context for a viable black ecclesiology.

Gabriel Settiloane provides an African perspective on the person and community in these words: "Man is man-in-community: motho ke motho ka batho—man is only man through other people."[11]

Herein lies the African "tribal mystique." This does not mean, according to Settiloane, "that the individual is submerged in his social environment. It does mean, however, that the locus of any individual must extend as far as the social activity of relationships which constitute it extends. For instance, the dead are believed to be with the living."[12]

Fasholé-Luke, writing on ancestors, observes, "We cannot simply say that African ancestors can be embraced within the framework of the universal Church and included in the Communion of Saints." He continues, "The phrase *sanctorum communio* (interpreted) to mean fellowship with holy people of all ages and the whole company of heaven through participation in the holy sacraments, gives us a signpost to the road on which our theologizing should travel."[13]

While black Christians do not seem to hold to this strong belief in ancestors, there is through their understanding of biblical faith a sustained belief in the reunion of families beyond death. This is dramatically presented on the occasion of the final rites for a deceased relative. The strong extended family instincts of African communal life appear forcefully at the time of bereavement. This common cultural aspect of the African and Afro-American connection could be the building material of a relevant doctrine of church and sacraments. It also provides a rich suggestion for the doctrine of last things.

Christology

While the entire system of Christian doctrine needs rethinking in the African as well as the Afro-American contexts, we have had to be selective. The final example will be in reference to Christology.

In contrast to Cone, I find this doctrine the most difficult to formulate. While there is much latent Christocentrism in African theology as well as in black theology, this Christocentrism must be "inclusive" if it is to be viable. The "exclusive" Christocentrism of Cone is inadequate for the contextualization of black and African theologies. This need implies serious conversation between theologians and sociologists and phenomenologists of religion.

Cone's instincts are still Barthian at this point. And even if Barth's theology can be called to witness for some ethicopolitical insights, it is a serious question whether his program allows for serious dialogue between Christianity and non-Christian religious expressions. The background of African traditional religions is central to both African and black theological reflection. Just as process theologians, such as John Cobb, are attempting to reconceive Christology in dialogue with Buddhists, black theologians will need to participate in the Africanization of Christian theology at its Christological center.

Any Western hermeneutic will prove to be inadequate for this task. We must look elsewhere for guidelines. While taking seriously Western historical-critical scholarship and the profound theological programs based upon this, we need to unlock the riches of black/African spirituality and culture in the way we develop a Christological proposal. I accept, for example, the confessional core of Christology summed up in D. M. Baillie's classic *God Was in Christ.* For me, the Jesus of history is the Christ of faith. Christ is the center of God's revelation, but the circumference of God's salvific revelation is in all of creation and all of history and among all peoples. God is with us in Christ. God meets us in Christ where we are ethnically and culturally. God is Lord of *each* people and yet Lord of all. Christology is particular and, at the same time, universal. Christ is not culturally captive in the West. He is incarnate among all peoples in the places where they live. When missionaries sang, "Jesus shall reign where'er the sun . . . ," they had in mind a white Jesus whose lordship would be over human beings of a darker hue in the Third World. They therefore, in too many instances, became colonizers for God.

Bishop Idowu clinches the point when he asks, "If Christ can speak British English and American, why can't he speak Yoruba, the language of my people?" A Japanese theologian, Koyama, writes, "There is no handle on the cross." We must now develop a christic understanding that is adequate for all people to cry out, "My Lord and my God." And yet the savior of each person and each people must be understood as the Redeemer of all humankind.

Conclusion

The context of black theology is temporally and spatially distinct from African theology, but they are linked by a common ancestry. Here one can claim too much and one can claim too little. What is important is to affirm what we have in common that is mutually enriching and together develop meaningful statements of doctrine for our people through critical and yet positive dialogue. To this conversation we invite all people of African descent—those in the West Indies and Latin America as well as blacks and Africans.

We can document from our cultures similarities of religious experience, liturgy, belief, and practice. Racism and colonialism have triggered similar problems of identity and suffering. Therefore the need for group consciousness and social, economic, and political change is too often similar. Thus our task of contextualizing the gospel at this time in world history must move forward with haste but with serious thought. Our people are on the move; deliverance is their goal. Those of us who have been called to the theological task must hasten to join them.

CHAPTER 4

Jesus and His Church

Christology and ecclesiology are two important doctrines in liberation theologies and in black theology in particular. The very nature of a theology concerned with liberation from oppression and reconciliation among those to be set free requires a careful examination of Jesus and his church. Christology needs reexamination in order to make sure that the historical Jesus is given due attention as well as the Christ of faith. Ecclesiology requires careful attention because of the importance of fellowship and community among those who are oppressed. There is another reason also to look seriously at the nature and mission of the church. The empirical gathering of Christians has a "political" mission as well as a therapeutic one.

In treating the subject matter of this chapter, we note that traditional theology can be greatly enriched by insights from various emphases in liberation theologies. Elsewhere I have used the image of the family (extended) in the African and Afro-American religious traditions to speak of the church.[1] Latin American liberation theology has been primarily "church theology." This is due partly to the preponderance of Roman Catholic writings among the pacesetters in that movement. But there is another equally important reason why this is so. Its target is classism, which is a form of structural evil. This form of evil can only be engaged and overcome by an opposing structure of righteousness and justice. Finally, feminist theologies can enrich all other understandings of the church of Jesus Christ because they seek to overcome sexism which is present in all earthly manifestations of the church.

The Jesus of History as the Christ of Faith

Jesus has always had a special place in black theology from the beginnings of Afro-American religious history. Jesus has been understood as a "friend" and "brother." What happened in his human

existence from "crib" to "cross" and beyond has been chronicled
in black sermons, in black songs and literature. It is interesting that
black thinkers have held to their affinity to the Jesus of history even
after the most intense exposure to biblical criticism.[2] The Jesus of
Howard Thurman is concerned about human beings who are oppressed.[3] Rosemary Ruether has captured a vision of Christology
that is shared by most programs of liberation theology. She speaks
of a holistic vision as she writes.

> For liberation theologians sin means not only alienation from God and
> personal brokenness of life, but also the structural evils of war, racism,
> sexism and economic exploitation which allow some people to dehu-
> manize others. Likewise salvation means not only reconciliation with
> God and personal amendment of life, but a commitment to a struggle
> for a transformed social order where all these evils will be overcome.[4]

Ruether, a feminist theologian, has given constant attention to
"an infra-structure" of oppressions to be addressed by all theologians of liberation. Thus it is not surprising that her reflections on
Christology provide a good context in which to look at Christology
as we project the future of black theology. Ruether is instructive as
she brings her perspective of feminism to Christology, but what we
have thus far referred to has value for all of Christology from a
liberationist point of view.

Several major works on Christology have now been developed by
Latin American liberation theologians. Their works are so impor-
tant for understanding faith in Jesus Christ that any examination of
Christology is now incomplete that does not investigate their works.
The contributions of Leonardo Boff, Jon Sobrino, and José Miranda
should be examined,[5] along with such writers as D. M. Baillie, Hans
Küng, Edward Schillebeeckx, Paul Tillich, and Karl Barth, among
others.

The relevance of the message of the Christological insights of
Latin American liberation theologies is apparent when one observes
that poverty and racism often occur together. To be victim of one
often leads to infliction by the other.

Boff reminds us that liberative praxis constitutes the surest road
to the God of Jesus Christ. He further implies that the liberative
nature of Jesus' activity shows up clearly in his social relationships.

> Justice occupies a central place in his proclamation. He declares that
> the poor are blest, not because he sees poverty itself as a virtue, but
> because poverty is the result of unjust relationships between human
> beings, provoking the intervention of the messianic king. The primary

function of this king is to do justice to the poor and to defend the rights of the weak.[6]

The designation of Jesus as liberator is used among liberation theologians to indicate Jesus' concern for the oppressed. This emphasis is different from the emphasis of those who speak only of Jesus as Lord. The lordship of Jesus is often associated with the Christ of faith and with Christian triumphalism. This is good news for those who are doing well in a material sense as well as those who are sure of their righteousness. What we believe about Jesus relates to our understanding of God as well. Jesus as liberator points to a God who shares our pain and poverty, our suffering in this world. Lordship, rightly understood, says something important about God. But Jesus as liberator says something about God who reveals himself in Jesus Christ, which we must not leave unspoken.

In his *Sanctorum Communio*, Dietrich Bonhoeffer has made the understanding of Jesus Christ central to the meaning of God, personhood, and community.[7] Even though the theology of Barth was influential to Bonhoeffer in his early writings, the latter's developing Christology took a different turn. Bonhoeffer was concerned about faith and community. His thought focused on this world with a view to concrete action. Christ remained, however, the center for our knowledge of this world as well as of the ultimate—God and the future life. Barth was concerned about faith and history (a spiritual and transcendent version of history). Christology for Barth was that which began with the cross, resurrection, and ascension of Christ. It took Barth many decades to finally discover the humanity of God. Bonhoeffer, on the other hand, began his career with a deep understanding of how the earthly life of Jesus provides a basis for Christology. We are just beginning to appreciate the magnitude of Bonhoeffer's contribution to what is being called liberation theology today. It is significant that John DeGruchy is drawing out the implications of Bonhoeffer's thought for apartheid in South Africa.[8] The seminal influence upon black theology is clearly due to the close ties between the context and content of black theology in the United States and South Africa.

Another person whose reflections on Jesus will enrich our discussion is John Yoder. Yoder, a Mennonite theologian who is professor of theology at Notre Dame, has provided a valuable study entitled *The Politics of Jesus*. This work brings New Testament studies and social ethics together with a concern for problems of power and revolution. Central to Yoder's understanding of Jesus is the text in the Gospel of Luke often quoted in theologies of liberation as a foundational text (Luke 4:14–15). Jesus, according to Yoder, quotes from Isaiah 61 and turns the meaning of the text upon himself.[9] The interpretation of Jesus that Yoder provides in the first three chapters helps us to overcome the Christ of dogma emphasis in much contemporary theology. The Jesus of Yoder's exposition points to the God of the exodus as well as the God of Easter. This God who meets us is concerned about bondage and freedom, pain and healing, despair and hope in our earthly pilgrimage. In a word, this is Jesus the liberator. But like Bonhoeffer, Yoder reminds us of the cost of discipleship and that grace is costly. Like black church theology, Yoder believes that "God will fight our battle" and that ultimately God through Jesus Christ has the last word in human history.[10]

As we conclude this statement on the Jesus who is the "foundation" of the church, we are again reminded that the Jesus of history is the Christ of faith. The life and ministry of Jesus, during the days of his flesh, is essential to a full assessment of how he is *from* God and *with* us. Incarnation and atonement are inseparably linked. What he does for us depends upon who he is in relation to God and to us human beings. The incarnation is the atonement. Christ is the center of everything for the Christian and he is the foundation of the church, his body.

How Shall We "Image" the Church?

The use of images or models in the theological interpretation of the church is but a means to an end. The church exists in two dimensions—visible and invisible. In a sense the Christian life has an earthly and a heavenly aspect. Language and concepts are inadequate to express fully the finite and the infinite at the same time. Faith often expresses itself through paradox and analogy. Against this background it is useful to use images as we attempt to understand better the nature and mission of the church of Jesus Christ.

Images of the church are varied. It may be that no one image can be filled with sufficient meaning to say all that needs to be said concerning the church. In order to derive meaning from any image of the church a great deal of exegesis and contextualization is required. The hermeneutical task is to determine what a particular image of the church *meant* and then assess what it *means* as we look at the nature and mission of the church today.

We need to search Scripture and tradition for suitable images for understanding the church. Liberation theologians (black as well as Latin American) have suggested a need for a new hermeneutical perspective. Luis Segundo as well as James Cone has suggested a hermeneutic of "suspicion." This method uses insights from Scripture and the "sociology of knowledge." It begins with Scripture, moves rapidly forward to the present situation, and then, upon careful analysis of the present situation, moves back to Scripture and from there to the present. Such is the interpretation of theological doctrines by means of the hermeneutic of suspicion.

There are both strengths and weaknesses in this method, which has been used by Segundo and Cone. It seems quite useful for a political hermeneutic, but it does not appear to be as useful if one desires a more cultural approach to theology. Since black theology is at once political and cultural, further reflection is needed to satisfy a more holistic perspective.

A contextualized "imaging" of the church will require a serious engagement with cultural history as well as with geopolitical realities. The image one uses should be as holistic as possible, chosen upon the basis of careful reflection.

Much of Latin American liberation theology comes out of the Roman Catholic theological tradition. This theology is essentially church theology, rooted in the theological understanding of the church. Other programs in liberation theology are often in the Protestant tradition. Only in Francophone Africa has a black Catholic theology surfaced. Black Catholics in the United States have yet to produce a strong theological spokesperson. The African French-speaking Catholic theology resembles Afro-American theology mainly on the cultural side with lack of emphasis on the political front.

I would therefore explain the similarity of Roman Catholic and Protestant Afro-American theology more on cultural grounds than on theological foundations. Black theology grew out of black consciousness and black power. It is concerned about the well-being of people who are the victims of racist oppression. This includes all aspects of existence as well as the life of the soul. Personal faith and spiritual and moral development are included, but there is much concern about all dimensions of life in this world. Martin Luther King, Jr., expressed this concern well in his first sermon at Dexter Avenue Baptist Church in Montgomery, Alabama. His sermon was entitled "The Three Dimensions of a Complete Life."[11]

Again, black theology is contextualized in the life of a community with all of its social, economic, political, and cultural aspects. Church membership, fellowship, ministry, and mission need to be "a family affair." The church as an institution touches upon the total life-world of the black community. The black church is on an errand for God within the context of black life-in-community. An oppressed people seeking a life of freedom should always be aware of the existence of persons-in-community. Its effective witness, for

liberation or reconciliation, is based upon its "corporate personality." A community in distress cannot rely on the individual witness
of Christians one by one. This important insight is biblical; it was
the nature of Old Israel as well as the foundation for the New Israel.
It is also African, since religious and social existence there is often
referred to by the word *ujamaa,* or "familyhood." The distinguished
black minister-educator, Benjamin Elijah Mays, often drove his plea
for black unity home with these words, "The strength of the wolf
is the pack, and the strength of the pack is the wolf." We are here
applying this truism to the imaging of the church in the black tradition. Our image of the church needs to incorporate our unity in
diversity, both our individuality and our community in fellowship
with each other and with Christ.

The writings of Avery Dulles and Paul Minear are useful in this
context in stating an understanding of the church. Dulles is a
Roman Catholic Jesuit theologian who has taught at Woodstock
College and Catholic University. Minear, a Protestant New Testament theologian, taught at Yale for most of his career. Both Dulles
and Minear have contributed to the project in which we are engaged, that of imaging the church.

Dulles[12] sees image thinking as crucial for a doctrine of the
church. He sees tradition as normative, beginning in Scripture and
continuing in the church fathers. Thus he claims two thousand years
of tradition supporting his use of images. The pragmatic reason for
images is also compelling. Dulles asserts that a large and continuing
society requires symbolism to hold it together. For an image to be
effective it must be functional as well as cognitive. It must be rooted
in the corporate experience of the faithful. Images are important for
the life of the church—its preaching, liturgy, and esprit de corps.

However, Dulles makes a distinction between the psychological
and the intellectual functions of images. Thus, images that are useful to the liturgist and preacher may be of limited value to the
theologian. But what if the theologian is also a liturgist and
preacher? The distinction may be useful for emphasis, but it should
never be absolute. If theology is rooted in praxis, this separation
would be impractical as well as improbable.

Again, Dulles distinguishes between "models" [13] that are *explanatory* and those that are *exploratory.* The *explanatory* model brings
together what we already know or are inclined to believe—it accords
with what history and experience tell us about the Christian life. An
example in ecclesiology would be the use made of the parable of the
wheat and the tares. Here one finds a description of the presence
of evil in the church. But such a botanical model (image) does not
account for the interpersonal and historical phenomena in the

church's life. Only a societal model such as the people of God in pilgrimage can do that.[14]

The *exploratory* model, on the other hand, leads to new theological insights. It facilitates an understanding of the church in its ongoing life. It may even reveal new aspects of the gospel. Dulles points to the Servant of God model of the church as a recent example of this latter model. It is based upon the biblical image of Israel and Christ as Servant of God, but at Puebla it led the Latin American church to a fresh understanding of its nature and mission.[15]

This important study by Avery Dulles has many helpful suggestions, and we are greatly in his debt for such a stimulating discussion. His concern for the social understanding of the church and his insights into various individual images, mixed metaphors, and paradigms of the church are fruitful for reflection.

Minear in many ways supplements and enriches Dulles from a biblical point of view. A black theology must be deeply rooted in Scripture. Minear's imaging of the church develops out of his New Testament studies. There is, Minear observes, discontinuity as well as continuity between the New Testament and the modern church. Image language is the more important because it often transcends changes in forms, concepts, and practices better than prosaic language.

We live in a different thought world from that of New Testament times. In the New Testament, priority was given to figurative meanings. We tend to substitute concrete terms for images. Our problem is to disentangle literal and figurative meanings. For example, we may use the word "temple." In the Bible it may at one time refer to an experience with God. The literal and figurative meanings are inseparable as they refer to the heavenly and earthly happenings associated with this one word "temple." The worldview of the definer is decisive in determining its meaning. Minear suggests that we accept the literal and the figurative meanings together as a given. He writes:

> Where thought is absorbed with realities that instinctively fuse God's activity with man's and that therefore combine heavenly and earthly components, there this thought, together with its channels will more often than not ignore any inflexible earth-bound distinction between the literal content and the figurative. Such thought will use without embarrassment images around which a whole galaxy of meanings revolves in orbit.[16]

Images, according to Minear, serve three purposes: (1) They perform a rhetorical purpose; (2) they enable us to perceive reality; and

(3) they provide self-understanding (for a person or a group).[17] The second and third purposes are most important for ecclesiology. In order to understand mystery the imagination must be awakened. And a person as well as a society is unhealthy if there is a conflict between its outward behavior and its self-image. The New Testament calls us to the depths of reality, to discover an authentic self-portrait at a level where human beings are made and unmade. The church needs to seek its own self-understanding. It needs to compare its present life with the purpose for which our Lord calls it into existence. The biblical images have been one means by which the church has sought and found self-knowledge. Our hermeneutical task is to discover the initial rootage and worldview of the images used in reference to the church and then appropriate their meaning in our present understanding.

Jesus and His Church: Implications for Black Theology

Adolf Harnack asserted that the belief that Jesus founded a church does not rest on a historical foundation.[18] In defense of the belief in Jesus' role in founding the church, Newton Flew provides a fivefold argument that deserves careful examination. First, the preaching of Jesus is directed to the reconstitution of Israel in view of the advent of God's rule. The little flock to which Jesus spoke was said to be the New Israel. Second, the ethical teaching of Jesus can be understood only as directed to this nucleus of the New Israel. It included the promise of God's power to enable the disciples to translate the teaching into life. Third, the conception of messiahship, as used by Jesus, implies the gathering of a new community. Fourth, the conception of word, gospel, or mystery which Jesus proclaims is regarded as the basis for the new community. The gospel involves the notion of a new covenant to be established with the newly constituted people of God; and, fifth, the mission of the new community is declared when Jesus sends forth his disciples.[19]

Beyond this, Flew traces the discussion of Jesus as founder of the church through Pauline writings, 1 Peter, Hebrews, Revelation, and the Fourth Gospel. His conclusion is that Jesus is the founder of the community called church—the ecclesia on earth is called to be in the purpose of God as revealed in Jesus Christ. The church is said to be God's own creation. The origin of the church lies in the will of God. But a new era was inaugurated by the Spirit as a result of the revelation of God in the whole work of Christ, in his earthly life, his suffering on the cross, and his resurrection. Those who accepted this revelation through Christ as a saving message entered the New Israel—God's universal ecclesia as manifested on earth. Those who accept membership in this sacred community live in the awareness of the New Israel. Flew writes:

> Already, the divinely given principle of fellowship into the Holy Spirit is being translated into the concrete life of the new community. . . . The church they know has been constituted through the work of the Incarnate Word of God, by the sharing in the Spirit, the preaching of the word, and the administration of the Sacraments.[20]

The Christian church was established by Jesus Christ and is an extension of the incarnation. It is a fellowship designed to carry out his saving mission in the world. The church has a ministry of liberation and reconciliation in a world experiencing bondage and estrangement both personal and social. Its mission is to heal and disturb. Its message is at once a healing balm and a word of judgment. Jesus, who is Lord of the church, is its priest and prophet. He leads the church onward toward God's kingly rule. The church militant moves toward the church triumphant, when the ecclesia of God will become the *basileia* of God in the summing up of all things.

This chapter has underscored the understanding of the church as secure within the Christian tradition, under the headship of Jesus Christ. If the church is viewed as an extension of the incarnation, then ecclesiology and Christology belong together.

Black theology brings, together with all theologies of liberation, a peculiar dimension to ecclesiology. It has a special concern for social transformation and the liberation of oppressed people. This means that image thinking regarding the church is useful. In *Roots of a Black Future*, I selected the family image of the church and attempted to state why this understanding of the church is powerful for the black church in its ministry and mission. Imaging the church as a body or as a community could be equally significant. The significance of the church as a corporate unity is the essence of this perspective. A structure of evil and injustice needs to be confronted by the structure of grace if social structures are to be transformed and humanized. Thus the insights of Avery Dulles and Paul Minear are especially helpful, as they treat models and images of the church.

The institutional church is usually more important in Roman Catholic theology than in Protestant theology. This may be why Dulles is so preoccupied with the church as a historic structure—as an organization that resembles other human societies. Much has to do with the authority ascribed to the church for faith and practice.

Liberation theologies may be centered in Scripture or Christology and yet have an equal concern for the church as a corporate body in visible form. Building upon the paradigms of the exodus, the corporate personality of Israel, and Jesus as liberator, these theologies see the gathered people of God as having a liberating mission in the world.

Since black theology has a holistic outlook, there is no neglect of the healing dimensions of the church. The black church is therapeutic in its mission to all sorts and conditions of human beings. The church is an agent of liberational reconciliation. Jesus the liberator is the head of the church as transformer of culture. This church is visible and invisible, militant and triumphant.

CHAPTER 5

The Holy Spirit
and Liberation

A theological discussion that takes contextualization seriously must consider the unique contribution of black church theology to the doctrine of the Holy Spirit.

> And we believe in the Holy Spirit, the Lord and Giver of Life, who proceedeth from the Father and the Son, who with the Father and the Son together is worshiped and glorified, who spoke by the prophets. And we believe one holy catholic and apostolic church. (Nicene/Constantinopolitan Creed)

Our focus here is on the relationship between the doctrine of the Holy Spirit and human liberation. What is the connection between charismata and personal and social transformation? The African and Afro-American holistic religious understanding does not endorse the Western-oriented division between the personal and the social or the physical and the spiritual. There is an assumed interpenetration in both instances. Thus we must consider how the nature, presence, and power of the Holy Spirit are to be understood in a meaningful way in the black church tradition.

Why the Black Theologian Must Discuss the Holy Spirit

There is much "Spirit talk" today. Many questions are being asked about this cardinal doctrine of the Christian faith. Recently I received a letter asking: "Why are not liberation theologians writing about the Holy Spirit? Is there no Spirit talk among the liberation theologians, black feminists, or Latin Americans?" My candid answer had to be that little direct attention has been given to this subject in the liberation theology literature. A black colleague of mine who has given much attention to the doctrine of the Holy Spirit readily agreed that the Holy Spirit had been neglected in recent black theology. But there is no gainsaying of the importance of the Holy Spirit in the black church tradition. If the worship among most blacks is satiated with the presence of the Spirit, the worship of the more cultured and educated blacks often suffers from the Spirit's absence. In both cases there may be a need for deeper understanding. The spirits must be tested to discern whether they are of God.

We may focus our discussion by the use of an example. Eldridge Cleaver, who wrote in the late 1960s a work entitled *Soul on Ice,* wrote a later book called *Soul on Fire.* [1] In the earlier period, Cleaver expressed forcefully the disenchantment that many black militants and intellectuals felt regarding the quietism of black religion. The black churches were seen as comfort stations and havens of escapism. Cleaver was quoted often by black militants who saw black religion and the churches as the last bastion of Uncle Tomism. When Cleaver wrote *Soul on Fire,* he represented the so-called "born again" company of blacks and whites who claim to have received a second blessing, the outpouring of the Spirit in their souls. The example of Cleaver, of black militants deprogrammed by religious fervor, is more widespread than we might want to admit. But what is more disturbing is the influx of young intellectuals, black faculty members and professionals as well as students, into highly emotional religious movements claiming the name of the Holy Spirit. Such movements are usually associated with an otherworldly outlook that does not fit the holistic orientation of the black church tradition.

When blacks turn away from a concern for the social, economic, and political aspects of liberation in their religious life, something unusual has been happening. We need to discuss the presence and power of the Spirit in the black church in the light of these concerns. Recognizing that the true Spirit of God bears clearly discernible "fruits" in the life of the believer, we will look at the doctrine of the Holy Spirit.

What Is the Holy Spirit?

We begin with the etymology of the word "spirit." The Hebrew *ruach,* the Greek *pneuma,* and the Latin *animus* refer to the movement of air. These words are often translated as "wind," "storm," or "breeze." Since the movement of the air may be caused by "breath," the metaphorical meaning shifts from "breath" to the "principle of life" or "vitality." Human beings and animals have *ruach,* but God preeminently has *ruach.* God is . breathing, living, and acting God. In creation, God bestows *ruach* upon the creatures. Human beings receive God's *ruach* to the highest degree—human life results from the breathing of God. Wherever God acts, *ruach* is at work. God's action as the presence and power of *ruach* is prevalent in the Old Testament.

The Greek New Testament continues the same basic meaning of Spirit. *Pneuma* is the sign of human vitality. Greek has two words for the human spirit: *nous,* which refers to "mind" or "intellect," and *pneuma,* which points to the dynamic principle of life. John writes, "The spirit blows *(pneuma pnei)* where it wills . . . ; so it is with every one who is born of the Spirit *(pneumatos)"* (John 3:8).

In sum, we may assert the following: Spirit means that God is a vital, acting God. God grants life and vitality to creation. The human *ruach/pneuma* is God's inspiring breath by which life is given in creation and re-creation. God is in action in human life. The *pneuma* of a human being is his or her *dynamis*—person in action. The *pneuma* of God is God acting in creation, providence, and redemption.[2]

Pneumatology and Christology

We need to see the Spirit in relation to our understanding of Jesus Christ. Hendrikus Berkhof's discussion is useful on this point. He sees a double relationship between the Spirit and Christ. In the first instance the Spirit is said to have a priority over Jesus. Jesus is described as the bearer of the Spirit. The Synoptic Gospels point up this relationship between Jesus and the Spirit. In accordance with the prophecies, it was expected that the Spirit would rest upon the Messiah. The Messiah would be anointed by God with the Spirit. This association of the presence and power of the Spirit with Jesus is illustrated by passages in Matthew, Luke, and Acts. This view is widespread throughout the New Testament. (See Matt. 1:20; 4:1; Luke 4:14; 10:21; Acts 1:2; 10:38; John 3:34; Rom. 1:4.)

Paul and John emphasize another relationship between the Spirit and Christ as well. Paul writes concerning the Spirit as the Spirit of Christ or the Spirit of the Son (Rom. 8:9; 2 Cor. 3:17; Gal. 4:6; Phil. 1:19). John writes that Christ refers to "the Counselor, the Holy Spirit, whom the Father will send in my name" (John 14:26), "whom I shall send to you from the Father" (15:26). In John 20:22 the risen Christ, by breathing on the apostles, transmits to them the Holy Spirit. Again the role of sender of the Spirit which is predominant in John and Paul is not absent from the Synoptic Gospels and Acts. See, for example, Luke 24:49 and Acts 2:33. These two relationships of Christ and the Spirit are complementary. Jesus is the sender of the Spirit because he has first been the receiver and bearer of the Spirit.[3]

Theologians have not held these two aspects of the doctrine of the Holy Spirit together. Those who seek to lift up the humanity of Jesus have stressed Jesus as bearer of the Spirit. On the other hand, those who exalt the divinity of Christ have stressed him as one who sends the Spirit as a gift to the church. This trend is clear from the Adoptionists at the end of the second century until the liberals of today.

It is important to develop a Christology from an understanding of the Spirit of God that combines these two relationships of Jesus as "bearer" and "sender" of the Spirit of God. From a reading of the Old Testament, we understand that Jesus Christ is to be what H. Wheeler Robinson refers to as "a corporate personality." The whole of Israel and even of humankind is summed up in Jesus as the Servant of the Lord, the Messiah, the Son of Man, the Last Adam. Jesus is conceived by the Spirit, guided by the Spirit, filled with the Spirit. The Spirit rests on Jesus and goes out from Jesus. The one on whom the Spirit remains baptizes with the Holy Spirit.

The early attempts to develop a Christology used this pneumatic approach. This tendency may be noted in the apostolic fathers, for example, Ignatius, Second Clement, and the fifth parable of the Shepherd of Hermas. Hermas asserts that the Holy Spirit, which existed before creation and which participated in the entire creation, God made to dwell in a flesh that God ordained. This enfleshment of the Spirit, according to Hermas, "served the Spirit well in a behavior of purity and virtue, without casting any stain on the Spirit."[4] Hermas assumes that the flesh, the human nature of Christ, after his earthly work, was exalted and elected to the fellowship of the Spirit.

Around the middle of the second century there is a moving away of Christology from pneumatology. Titianus in his "Speech Against the Greeks" (ca. A.D. 65) used *ruach* ("spirit") and *dabar* ("word") as almost synonymous. But even so his discussion is a key turning point in which Christian apologists began to prefer *logos* ("word") rather than *pneuma* ("spirit") as their foundational concept. *Logos* was a popular philosophical concept at the time. The use of this later concept made the gospel more acceptable for the intellectual contemporaries of these theologians. Thus pneumatic Christology was replaced by logos Christology. But reliance upon Hellenistic cosmology distorted the biblical basis for Christology and led to its impoverishment. Logos Christology prevailed and is the essence of the church's Christological formulations. It is important, therefore, to ask whether we should not reassess pneumatic Christology and its support in the biblical record.[5] Only by relating pneumatology to Christology and holding a Christological view of pneumatology may we come to a sound doctrine of the Holy Spirit.

The Holy Spirit and the Second Blessing

We need to ask whether Pentecostalism today is consistent with the outpouring of the Spirit at Pentecost. Another way of raising the issue is to ask whether baptism in the Holy Spirit is distinct from conversion. Is it a second blessing? Are those who believed themselves to be true Christians but who have no evidence of a second blessing deceived? Even if they live a Christian life-style, must they feel inferior if they have not received the gift of speaking in tongues? Have those who believe they have received the second blessing the right to judge the deficiency in others or feel superior in comparison to those who have not been thus favored by God? These questions are crucial because blacks are often emotional in their religious cult expression and are greatly attracted to the Pentecostal movement.

The Pentecostal movement believes that it has found in the acts of the apostles, in its evangelical forebear, and in its own personal and missionary experience precedent and authority for its basic belief. Pentecostals assert that baptism in the Holy Spirit is a critical experience subsequent to and distinct from conversion, granting the believer the benefits of a permanent, personal, and full indwelling of the Holy Spirit. The believer thus receives power for Christian service, particularly evangelistic service, and the equipment of spiritual gifts.

Frederick Bruner describes the experience of the second blessing at the center of Pentecostalism. "A Christian is believed to be given personal graces . . . as a result of his initial faith, but the ministering gifts, the charismata (e.g., I Cor. 12:8–10) are not fully given until the latter bestowal."[6]

Certain conditions are necessary both to explain and to obtain baptism in the Holy Spirit with its glossolalic evidence. Supporters of the doctrine find in Acts and in other biblical passages a connection between the gift of the Spirit and conversion, obedience, prayer, and faith. Again Bruner provides a helpful account (*A Theology of the Holy Spirit*, pp. 114–115):

> Conversion is the dispensable pre-condition for the Pentecostal baptism. Obedience—both active (with the goal of the sinless heart) and passive (with the goal of self-emptying)—is the Christian's essential preparation for the baptism in the Holy Spirit. When the obedience is complete the Christian should have faith. The faith which Pentecostalism prizes in this connection is not usually identical with initial Christian faith; it is a different kind or at least a different act of faith, directed primarily toward the Holy Spirit with a quantitative intensity, and is as such neither *sola* nor *simplex*. It is a faith added to a prepara-

tory commitment necessary for acquiring and for appreciating the gift of the Holy Spirit. Pentecostal faith is best described as *ultima fides.*

Bruner is also very helpful in regard to the Pentecostal claim that the evidence of a second blessing replaces the demand for circumcision in the early church. Paul confronted forthrightly this party at Corinth with a rejoinder. (See 1 Cor. 12:1–13:2.) Judaistic evidence of circumcision and the Pentecostal evidence are supplements to initial faith and are required to receive God's favor and/or power in a complete sense. Likewise they are momentary physical phenomena, occurring at specific bodily organs, and both seem to have guaranteed, as it were, *ex opere operato,* the reality that each purports to verify. That is to say, in both cases the physical event is invested with spiritual importance.[7]

There is a distinct danger. The supplement to faith easily becomes faith's center. This was true of the "circumcision party" in Paul's days (Gal. 2:12) as well as of the "tongues movement" today. The supplement to faith becomes more important than faith and claims to be a higher type of Christian experience. Bruner's concern is, therefore, that any supplement to faith cancels "the sole necessity of faith." Christ is no longer sufficient in his atoning work. Faith sealed in baptism is no longer adequate. This view of the role of the Spirit renders the saving power of the cross and the gospel empty. It is salvation by works rather than by faith alone.[8]

Bruner's critique is well taken up to a point, but the distinction he makes between faith and works, God's grace and human responsibility, is disturbing. To use a metaphor, the cure is worse than the sickness. Does not redemption have both human and divine dimensions? Faith and works are interdependent. The concerns of Bruner regarding Pentecostalism are echoed by Paul Opsahl, from the Lutheran point of view. Again faith and works and law and gospel are juxtaposed.[9] In both cases, inadequate attention is given to ethics and social responsibility. In the case of Pentecostalism we are dealing with a supplement to saving faith that is questionable. But in the critique of Bruner and Opsahl we are introduced to a concept of faith that is incomplete—it leaves out ethics, especially a "public ethic."

In Pentecostalism the indwelling Spirit or the second blessing is the result of sinlessness, prayer, obedience, and the laying on of hands. Holiness is viewed not as growth toward spiritual maturity but as sinlessness. Obedience is absolute and takes little notice of human free will as essential to selfhood. Those receiving the second blessing have a privileged stance—a kind of inside track on God's grace. Other Christians and churches are in a second-best position.

Pentecostalism is for the "twice-born," not for those who experience the life of faith as a still small voice or a gradual experience of sanctification, however saintly the life.

In spite of all its emphasis upon personal moral perfection, the virtues of Pentecostalism are often negative and private. It is notoriously short on social conscience and social justice. Corporate sins are seldom recognized, and there is little concern for social transformation. Thus my objection to the claims of Pentecostalism is based upon ethical rather than purely evangelical grounds. I do not have a problem with a faith that includes works as long as it has a gospel foundation—that is to say, as long as God and human beings are co-laborers together for good. A nontheistic humanism is not adequate. But I do seriously question the claim to a superior knowledge of God by any individual or group. Furthermore, this claim is too often accompanied by more heat than light—a zeal not always according to knowledge—or a less than exemplary moral life. There should be a relationship between *root* and *fruit* both in the private life and in the public domain.[10]

Pentecostalism: A Critique from Black Theology

Two criticisms of Pentecostalism have been made by black theologians. One relates to the question of how the power claimed for the church can be applied to the need of the people. Bennie Goodwin puts his concern this way: "The question facing Pentecostals is: How can the power that is continually experienced within the church fellowship be brought to bear on problems God's children are continually experiencing outside the church?"[11] The other question relates to what James Tinney calls the "exclusivist tendencies in Pentecostal self-definition."[12] Tinney argues that certain tongues-speaking denominations that have had more access to wealth and mass media have launched an effective, exclusivistic campaign to define Pentecostalism in a very narrow theological, racial, and cultural sense. In a word, he is concerned about the racism that has infested the Pentecostal movement.

We will deal first with Tinney's concern. If racism had not infiltrated the ranks of Pentecostalism, its social consciousness might have developed along more positive lines.

First, racism in Pentecostalism is *historical.* When the Azusa Street revival in Los Angeles was only a month old, white Pentecostals levied accusations against W. J. Seymour and his black followers. Whites claimed that Charles Parham's Topeka, Kansas, glossolalic event was the real genesis of authentic Pentecostalism in this country. The history of the movement is aimed at making white Pentecostals the only legitimate bearers of the title. Black writers view the matter differently. Leonard Lovett writes:

> The twentieth century Pentecostal Movement in America originated from the womb of the black religious experience. From a converted livery stable in the ghetto on Azusa Street in Los Angeles in 1906 to the world, the Pentecostal Movement has ushered in the era of the Holy Spirit. Once again God has used a "saving moment" from the ranks of the despised and oppressed people of the earth to inject new life and power into the church universal.[13]

It is not so much the genesis of the movement that bothers the black writers. It is, rather, the rejection of the authenticity of the black movement by the whites and their blatant attempt to overlook it. The assumption that only the white movement is legitimate and blacks are a part of it concerns the black Pentecostals. A case in point is that white writers stress that Seymour was a disciple of Parham, but they like to ignore the fact that many white ministers were ordained by Bishop Charles H. Mason, founder of The Church of God in Christ. White writers also like to speak of interracial fellowship. But how can one refer to sincerity of true fellowship when whites refused to defy laws, mores, and prejudices and serve under black leaders?[14]

Second, racism has influenced the *theology* of Pentecostalism. The accepted theological position is that scriptural revelation is final and without error among most white Pentecostals. Not only is reason doubted but even the Spirit is not trusted to lead to any new truth. Yet it is just at this point that black and African tongues-speaking bodies depart from "orthodoxy." Claims to new revelations are frequent and often figure into the formation of new organizations. Black Pentecostals have been formulating a black theology for a long time. They have relied on oral traditions, African cultural retentions, and the like. Blacks join African, Latin American, and Asian tongues groups in rejecting the definition of whites. Whereas whites limit themselves to a fundamentalist-evangelical theology, others find it inappropriate to subscribe to this exclusivistic self-definition.[15] Lovett writes, "Authentic Pentecostal encounter cannot occur unless liberation becomes the consequence. It is another way of saying no man can experience the fullness of the Spirit and be a racist."[16]

Third, white Pentecostalism is racist in an *institutional* sense. The superiority of whites over blacks is promoted by Pentecostalism in several ways. There is segregation in the organizations and their wider alliances. Whites have fled the inner cities and have often sold their properties for a handsome profit. The congregations that remain are often securely under white control. Blacks are relegated to subordinate positions, the image of Christ is white, and the illustrations used in Sunday school literature are all white. White Pentecostalism is anti-Third World as well. It traces its lineage to the Wesleys, Luther, and even to Palestine, but there is no reference to any African heritage.[17]

We now look briefly at the critique of Pentecostalism by black theology from the perspective of social consciousness. Theological spokespersons for the black Pentecostals see the need for the social outreach aspect of the gospel. The Spirit descends like a dove but also comes as wind and fire to liberate from oppressed conditions such as racism and poverty. James Forbes boldly writes concerning "progressive Pentecostalism." He does not discount the personal benefits of the Pentecostal experience. It restores a sense of worth, identity, and God-relatedness to persons who come out of loneliness, lostness, meaninglessness, and a crisis of identity. Persons experience joy, peace, healing, and personal freedom when exposed to the Spirit's influence.[18] But there will also be the expectation of spiritual gifts by which one can fight the forces of evil and promote the cause of the kingdom. Forbes goes even farther. He asserts that the church, under the inspiration of the Holy Spirit, will offer counseling for personal healing and, at the same time, will seek the aid of agencies for social welfare.

Progressive Pentecostalism relies firmly on the power of the Holy Ghost, according to Forbes. But it is "progressive" because it goes beyond institutional or denominational narrowness. It does not hold that the Spirit works in only one or two ways or only in a supernatural manner. Every human or divine activity that serves the realization of the kingdom of God is the concern of the Holy Spirit. The Spirit works outside as well as inside the organized churches. The Spirit's work is not limited to individual souls and "spiritual things." Anything that affects our attainment of an abundant life and social freedom is on the Spirit's agenda. Finally, according to Forbes, the Spirit is not bound by the past. The Spirit moves us into an open and new future.[19]

Goodwin is even more forceful and to the point:

> The times in which we live demand more than people jumping around in a church, lifting their hands and saying, "Praise the Lord" in an unknown tongue. The times demand that we speak with power to the powerful in a known tongue. The times demand that we discover where the power is trying to express itself in us, and that we develop that expression. We must take our places among the powerful and

devote the God-given Pentecostal power within us to the liberation of
the poor, the broken-hearted, the oppressed, the blind and the
bruised.[20]

In essence, then, black Pentecostals have called attention to the
racism that has splintered the Pentecostal ranks. It has provided a
very perceptive critique of the authenticity of the fellowship, theology, and practice of white Pentecostalism. The "fruits of the Spirit"
are absent in regard to the humanity of blacks and the poor. What
can we say concerning the source of such Pentecostal manifestation? With all of its fervent claims to the outpouring of the Spirit
in the individual soul, there is little evidence of concern for making
life more human for the oppressed. Usually where there is oppression based upon race and class, sexism is in the wings. This critique
of this movement by black theologians may be a service to the entire
church after all.

The Spirit and the Church

We are now prepared to look at the black church in "the power
of the Spirit." While the Spirit has had a central place in the black
church tradition, there has been a virtual neglect of this doctrine by
black theologians.

There needs to be serious theological development of many of
the insights of the black Pentecostal scholars. The Spirit has had
expression in a powerful way in most black denominations. It would
be valuable to trace the African roots of Pentecostalism among
blacks as well as the obvious universal impact of modern black
Pentecostal expression.[21] But the place to begin has to be in the
primitive Christian church and the witness of the Spirit in the whole
church of Christ.

The church as a creation of the Spirit is both an institution and
a community. Institutions belong to the world of structures. Communities belong to the world of persons. In the church, institution
and community, institute and event, are interrelated. *Institution* refers to established relationships and patterns of historical and social
order—stable forms and definite structures. *Event* points to the
energizing of the church by the Spirit, the spontaneous quality of
the human response and the character of the community's life of
grace. The event is foundational. The institutional elements are the
result and the vessel for the event. Berkhof states the case well:

> This institutional element and the community element are related to
> one another as root and fruit. The root is prior to the fruit, but the

fruit is the end as the root is the base. The metaphor is valid also insofar as the fruit comes and vanishes and the root is the basic and remaining element, thanks to which new fruits grow again and again.[22]

The church, the Spirit, and Christ are interrelated as follows:

> In Word, sacraments and ministry, Christ is made present to the community of his church. This community in its turn is called to be the means by which Christ is made present to the world. . . . The institute is not the first root—that is Christ himself. And the community is not the last aim—that is humankind as a whole. So the Spirit draws wider and wider the circles around Christ. The church is somewhere in the middle between Christ and the universe, as a partial realization of his goal and as a representative of his deeds and purposes toward the world. The unity of these two aspects is the nature of the church.[23]

The black church tradition illustrates the relationship of the church as event to the church as institute. The black church is operating in the power of the Spirit which moves from worship to social involvement, as it has frequently done throughout its history. Major Jones is perceptive as he writes concerning the church as "event." He sees the gathered church as event, but he does not establish a proper connection between the church as event and as institute. Thus he has a problem providing a theological basis for his ethics and ends up with "an ethic of distress." Just as the "event church" comes and goes, even so a Christian, when faced with tough moral choices, does not take his or her faith into action. One leaves one's faith by the way, according to Jones, does what has to be done, and then returns to reclaim one's faith.[24] Martin Luther King, Jr., moved from the church as event to the church as institute. His theology was the foundation for his social activism, whether or not we agree completely with either King's ethics or theology. It is consistent with the black church tradition to assert that the same Spirit that is present when the community is gathered also sends black Christians forth to claim their humanity. The Spirit that comforts and heals in black worship renews and empowers us as we oppose the evils in the society that would humiliate and destroy us.

Jürgen Moltmann's explorations into what he calls "a messianic ecclesiology" assert that the church as a messianic fellowship depends upon the presence and power of the Holy Spirit. He writes:

> The church is a means of salvation, through proclamation, baptism, the Lord's Supper, worship, prayer, acts of blessing and the center for individual comfort and corporate fellowship. But, on the other hand, the church consists of *charismata*, ministries, gifts and tasks which flow

from this fellowship into society. These "means of salvation" and these ministries are for the purpose of the role of the church as a messianic fellowship in the world . . . a messianic fellowship of service for the Kingdom of God.[25]

Black Christians have always been concerned about the relationship of the Spirit's presence and power to what happens between persons and not merely to what happens inside them. The Holy Spirit of God seems to have the greater interest in relationships between human beings. The Beatitudes in Matthew 5 and "the fruits of the Spirit" in Galatians 5 are inherent in the gospel, and their presence is an indication of the Spirit's presence and power. Even where the second blessing is important to black Christians, social justice is sought also. In the words of Samuel Rayan, "The Holy Spirit is in truth the Father of the poor, the one who is really concerned with the less fortunate and the marginated."[26]

Conclusion

We began our discussion of the Holy Spirit by noting how important the Spirit's presence and power is in the black church tradition. We then attempted to offer a working definition of the Holy Spirit. We found that it was essential to relate Christology to our discussion of the Holy Spirit. Christ both bears and sends the Spirit. When the Spirit is examined to determine its source, we understand the Holy Spirit in concert with the revelation of God in Jesus Christ. We looked at the claim of Pentecostals regarding the second blessing and questioned the authenticity of this in view of the "gifts" that the Spirit bestows upon all Christians to minister in Christ's name. Black Pentecostals, we observed, have made telling criticism of the privileged, exclusive, and racist character of white Pentecostalism. Their observations have been helpful in pointing to the manner in which blacks understand the presence and power of the Spirit. The Spirit not only heals; the Spirit empowers for liberation from oppression. And finally, we saw the church as *event* and *institute.* The Spirit-filled community, the family of God, is empowered for a messianic witness and ministry to hasten the coming of God's kingdom. In sum, in the black church tradition, the Spirit is not merely a dove but wind and fire also. The Comforter is also the Strengthener. Justice in the social order no less than joy and peace in the hearts of believers is, for the black church, evidence of the Spirit's presence and power.

CHAPTER 6

Love as Costly Grace

The next three chapters will deal with an extensive view of theological ethics. As a discipline, theological ethics is interdisciplinary in method. In this approach, one can draw upon contributions made by several cognate disciplines, such as systematics, ethics, philosophy, social science, history, and biblical studies. More and more we must also be sensitive to the relationships and effects of world cultures and geopolitical systems as well as religions in all cultures.

The comprehensive methodology in theological ethics is matched by subject matter. We are concerned about what makes life more human in every place and time. We are to remember that the cultural and institutional aspects of theological ethics are supported by a profound concern for the well-being of persons as individual selves. For instance, the contributions of Sigmund Freud and Søren Kierkegaard, no less than Karl Marx, must be appropriated to the task. The holistic perspective is at home in the Third World as it is among blacks, Amerindians, and Asians living in the West, to name a few. We are being compelled by circumstances to think inclusively in our pluralistic context. The percentage of Third World people in the population of the United States is rapidly increasing. In this situation, the wealth and power of Anglo-Saxon Protestants, Catholics, and Jews may not suffice to keep other cultural rumblings from being heard. The tide of history is sweeping inevitably toward pluralism and holism.

With this perspective before us, we turn to concepts that are not new. They are ancient and belong to the very foundations of religious, biblical, and philosophical thought in the West. This trilogy of love, justice, and power has been discussed many times by notable scholars in several disciplines. The concepts have been discussed separately, and in some cases love and justice have been treated together. Again, love, justice, and power have been compared. While I cannot start *de novo*, I am attempting to bring a

certain newness of perspective to the discussion of these classical
themes. We now raise the issue: What is the meaning and significance of love, justice, and power in this time and place?

The Meaning of Love

Love in the Old Testament is fundamentally a spontaneous feeling that leads to self-sacrifice. It is a personal force. The ultimate
ground of the idea is found in the love of person for person when
the word is used in a religious sense. The statement that God is love
implies personality. Even the covenant is an expression in juridical
terms of the experience of God's personal love. Attempts are made
in the Old Testament to associate love with various legal terms such
as mercy, judgment, and truth. There is the command on one hand
to love God and on the other the assertion that God loves us.

The message of love in the Old Testament is addressed both to
the people and to the individual. More is said in the Old Testament,
however, concerning God's love of the nation than regarding love
for a particular individual. Hosea stands out as having an unusual
insight into God's love. He clearly recognizes the flowing forth of
divine love at the heart of the election of Israel and the forming of
the covenant. Isaiah and Jeremiah closely approach Hosea in their
description of love.[1]

The Hebrew word *'ahebh* can mean the passion that unites hus-
band and wife (S. of Sol. 8:6-7), the unselfish loyalty of friends (1
Samuel 20), or devotion to righteousness (Ps. 45:7). God's love for
Israel is not instinct but will (Deut. 7:13); and the love of God for
humankind enjoined upon Israel is not ecstasy but service.

The essential characteristic of love in Israel is its tendency toward
exclusiveness. In the Old Testament, love is jealous—it chooses one
object among many and holds it fast with all the strength of its
passion and its will, brooking no relaxation of the bond of loyalty.
God has set many people in the world but gives God's love to the
elect nation. With this love, God makes a covenant that is loyally
kept and jealously guarded as if it was a bond of marriage (Hosea
1 ff.). To break the law is a breach of faith; to worship strange gods
is adultery, calling forth the passionate jealousy of Yahweh (Exodus
20).

The principle of loving one's neighbor is marked by the same
motif of exclusiveness. It is a love that makes distinctions, choosing,
preferring, rejecting—not a cosmopolitan love, embracing millions.
The Israelites begin their social activity at home, loving Israel first
as God does and bestowing their love upon the stranger who is
admitted for membership in their house or nation. The scope of

social responsibility is thus always defined in terms of a particular organism and a concrete situation.[2]

Before moving into the New Testament, we must give some attention to the Greek words for love. *Eros* was a sensual, demonic, and uncontrollable force. In the mysticism of Plotinus, *eros* was sublimated and became the overwhelming desire for union with the One. *Philia* indicated a liking or caring for others, divine or human. It denoted the love of friend for friend. Outside the New Testament, *agapē* often meant no more than to be content with something or to welcome someone with a courteous greeting. It had a deeper meaning when it indicated a liking of something or someone, sometimes meaning to place one value above another.

Turning to the New Testament itself, we find the idea of love most commonly expressed in the term *agapē*. *Agapē* in the New Testament is a love called out of one's heart by the preciousness of the object loved. It is a love devoid of sensuousness, the noblest word for love in the Greek language. *Agapē* was perhaps adopted by the New Testament writers because of its infrequent use and indefinite meaning in classical Greek. They were able to pour additional meaning into it by means of the contexts in which they used it. Thus the word, when used in the New Testament, refers to a love that impels the one loving to deny self for the benefit of the one loved.[3]

In Rabbinic Judaism love has an important place, but righteousness continues to provide the foundation of Jewish theology and ethics. It was Jesus who first broke down the old foundation walls and undertook the daring task of complete rebuilding. Jesus summarized the meaning of the old and the new righteousness in two sentences: "You shall love the Lord your God" and "You shall love your neighbor" (Mark 12:28–31; Matt. 22:36–40). Both are well-known sayings in Judaism and in Christianity. The new formula for neighborly love that Jesus set up differs from Hillel's famous rule by being positive. Hillel had said: "Do not unto thy neighbor what is hateful unto thee." Jesus stands clearly and consciously in the line of the Jewish ethical tradition. But Jesus demands love with such exclusiveness that all other commandments are included in it; love is the final criterion of righteousness. For Jesus, love is an affair of willing and doing. Our Lord presents love as a new demand. Jesus sets the love ethic free from its limitations to fellow nationals and brings it to bear upon all humanity. He takes the question out of the sphere of legal controversy and puts it in the heart.[4]

Jesus does not only proclaim a new demand, he creates a new order. He proclaims the divine mercy, not as the temper in which God always acts, but experienced as an unparalleled event, the possibility of which is grounded in God alone. He brings forgiveness of sins. When persons experience that, a completely new power of overflowing love is released within them. God in Christ has, by his act of forgiveness, introduced a new order into the world, which entirely surpasses the old, doing away with its scale of values, and creating new tasks and possibilities. The new relationship of God to humanity lays the foundation for a new relationship of person to person.

Rudolf Bultmann's reflections are instructive:

> Love does not mean an emotion which quickens the spiritual life and makes it sensitive, but a definite attitude of will. In reality the love which is based on emotions of sympathy, on affection, is self-love; for it is a love of preference, of choice, and the standard of preference and choice is the self. Friendship and family love are expressions of the natural self; they are as such neither good nor evil; they are bad when the will is bad. But to see in them the fulfillment of God's command to love is to falsify this command and to set self-love in the place of obedient love of neighbor. For the neighbor is not this or that man with whom I feel a bond of sympathy, it is every man; yet not every man in general, but every man with whom I come in contact. The command is you must love; the will is called to action. . . . The man is addressed with the implication that he is placed by God under the necessity of decision and must decide through his free act. Only if love is thought of as an emotion is it meaningless to command love; the command to love shows that love is understood as an attitude of will.[5]

According to Paul, the love of God is one with the love of Christ (Rom. 8:39). God's loving work is revealed in Christ: the eternal love of God becomes a redeeming event. The aim of God's love is the new humanity in Christ. But this is not achieved without loving action on the part of human beings. God produces in us that kind of life which makes us really responsible human beings. The purpose of divine love is that a person who is called in love and forgiveness should serve the neighbor. Paul views love as in the cross. Love is the willingness to serve and sacrifice, to forgive and make allowances, to share and sympathize, to lift up the fallen and restore the erring community. The community of faith owes its whole existence to the mercy of God and the sacrificial death of Christ.[6]

According to The Letter of James, faith grows strong through its activity in love. Love is the law of the new age—the royal law. This love is an act of faith and involves one's duty to the neighbor. To John, the chief function of the Son is to mediate God's love. The Son loves those whom the Father has given him. The Johannine *agapē* is a heavenly reality that comes down into the world. But this cosmic reality effects its revelation and achieves its victory in moral action. The world of light and life breaks through into this world in the form of love. Love for the neighbor springs from God and has its prototype in Christ. In the love of other persons the circle that consists of the Father and the Son and those who belong to the Father becomes a fellowship that is not of this world. God's love is life's ultimate reality. Love is a movement of life, a form of existence, a realization of God in this world. Love is the commandment that includes all others.[7] Thus in the biblical period, especially in the New Testament, love is a costly grace.

Augustine welded concepts of love from Christianity and Platonism into what he termed *caritas.* In his concept of *caritas,* Augustine allowed for human response and responsibility. God's grace is prevenient but not automatic. Luther rejected this concept,[8] holding that justification is not a righteousness from us or in us but a righteousness from God. However, Augustine's *caritas* provides for evangelical zeal but not at the expense of personal response and social responsibility. The love ethic must have a human dimension as well as a divine dimension. In its application, we as human beings must be laborers together with God for a just social order.

Love as Costly Grace

Love must be incorporated into the moral order. Unless high standards are set for the exercise of love, it can become trite and sentimental. In our day, love is often cheapened as *pity.* We are concerned about the homeless and the hungry, but often our concern is only to the extent that we will provide them a cot to sleep on at night and a hot meal now and then. I was in a meeting when a group of Atlanta ministers met with Mayor Andrew Young to talk about what the city could do to help the poor. As a newcomer to Atlanta, I was able to observe the situation with some objectivity. I noticed that the white ministers were very vocal about what they were doing to help the poor. The black ministers had little to say. In fact, many of the black ministers who were deeply involved in the urban ministry were not present. The white ministers spoke mainly of feeding the hungry and clothing the naked. They also provided places for the homeless to sleep in some downtown churches. They did not understand why the black ministers were so silent since those they sought to help were so often black. There was even a kind of self-righteousness about their reports.

What they did not speak about were jobs, houses, education, and general human rehabilitation. They did not address the unequal distribution of wealth in the city. They did not address the issue of how economic and political power could be exercised so as to make life more human. We cannot ask the right Christian theological question about the love ethic of Jesus unless we show concerns about the redemption of the social order that are equal to the outbursts of charity we show toward individuals. The love ethic of the Gospels is not limited to feeding the hungry, clothing the naked, and visiting the prisoner. It requires that we challenge unjust power structures to see that they are humane. We have a moral obligation to resist collective evil as well as to alleviate personal pain. To enter into this stubborn realm of "immoral society" is to invite cross-bearing. Love as charity is expected. We are often rewarded for social service. But when we challenge the sinful social structures and enter into the arena of social transformation, we may be marked for martyrdom. We run the risk that the system may break us. Many good people are absorbed into an evil system by their quietism and silence. These unwittingly become instruments of the evil system they deplore. A drum major for justice, as Dr. King called himself, often must "tread the winepress alone" as our Lord did. Genuine love is a costly grace. Dietrich Bonhoeffer did not merely write about this type of love, he experienced the pain of daring to live by that creed.

With the emphasis on praxis in liberation theology, there is no way to think of love in a meaningful sense without the possibility of solidarity in suffering with the oppressed. Martin Luther King, Jr., prepared the way for recent black theology programs by linking love inseparably with justice. Feminist theologians have reminded both liberation and black theologians that sexism is alive and well in their midst as they speak so loudly against oppressions based on class and race. Yet since most feminist theologians are white, they need to invite nonwhite feminist theologians into their ranks to speak for themselves. For example, black, Amerindian, Asian, and Hispanic women often suffer a triple oppression of class, race, and sex. What this means is that all liberation theologians need to look beyond a single issue of oppression. There is clearly an infrastructure of oppressions. At the same time that we call for liberation from our oppression, we need to be sensitive and responsible as we reach out to others who are also oppressed. This should help us to seek the liberation of the oppressor as well. In all of these concerns the meaning of love as a costly grace will be more adequately understood.

Love as costly grace requires that we love ourselves. At first, we could assume that self-love is the easiest form of love. One can love one's self, we would think, by merely deciding to do so. But suppose one's life is confused, meaningless, and without joy. Many people find themselves with much to live *on* but nothing to live *for*. They dread today and fear tomorrow. Their anxieties are pathological and they have tendencies toward self-destruction. As long as they are busy at work or caught up in social or recreational activities, they can make it. But they cannot live with self. They hate themselves whenever they are alone. As selfish as they are, the most dreadful thing in life is to look at themselves in a mirror. Sin, as self-centeredness, dominates their life, but self-hatred is the source of their misery. The most difficult love of all may be the love for a loveless self.

Yet there can be no genuine love for others that does not stem from self-love. What this means is that the fundamental task is the transformation of a loveless self to a self worthy of love. Here we do not mean selfishness or self-centeredness. When one wraps self in itself it is not only a small package, it is diminished and distorted; it becomes its own source of disaffection. The self is only fulfilled as it reaches out to other selves and to God. This is where divine aid as well as human community comes to the rescue of the self lost in its self-destruction. Tillich made a classic observation—that God's grace makes us acceptable even though we are unacceptable. That is to say that when we find our sins and wrongdoings so abundant that we have lost respect for ourselves and have begun to hate ourselves, God's grace transforms us into "new beings." As Christians we are re-created by divine grace. Self-love as used here therefore means self-acceptance.

This human nature which is reborn by God's act of re-creation is the basis for self-love. Self-love implies the affirmation that we are dignified persons with worth bestowed upon us by God in both creation and redemption. God is the divine parent and we are sons and daughters of this divine person by grace. Only through this awareness of personal worth may we enter into a quality relationship with others. A moral love of others is based upon the fact that we are able to love ourselves. Without this, the Golden Rule is not operable. The proper love of self determines the proper love of others.

Augustine referred to the *imago Dei* ("image of God") as the common ground for the love ethic. This is a good insight and is foundational to a sound affirmation of the Christian love ethic. That is to say, the *amor Dei* ("love of God") is primary. The love of God is essential to the love of the self and the love of others. When we love God we love the image of God in all human beings—ourselves and others. Augustine knew well that this image has been marred by sin and must be restored by grace. This latter reminder is essential to Christian ethical practice. It reminds us always that human beings are loveless as well as lovable. But the possibility of grace also provides us with patience and hope.

The love of self is a costly grace, as we have seen, but even so is the love of neighbor, particularly since our enemy is also our neighbor. The neighbor may be either friend or foe.

The love for those who love us appears to be easy. It would seem to be a simple matter to love close friends and members of our family. Yet this sometimes becomes our greatest burden. It is often very difficult to maintain integrity of character and a sense of personal purpose without breaking the most intimate personal ties. A Christian who decides to love God first may find his or her self forsaken by friends as well as foes. An estrangement may also develop with one's parents and other relatives. Love is never a cheap grace.

The love of the enemy is difficult indeed. The enemy is a self with freedom and will. How is it possible to change an enemy into a friend? Does love have the power to do this? How does one maintain love for oneself and express love for one's enemy at the same time? The love of the enemy is a requirement of the Christian love ethic. But how can we be faithful in the act of loving the enemy? The enemy can be evil and brutal in relating to us. Do we have the right of self-defense? If we exercise the right of self-defense, how then can we express love? Mahatma Gandhi and Martin Luther King, Jr., are among persons who sought an answer to these hard questions. They chose the way of nonviolence. Many assumptions were behind this choice: that we can distinguish between human worth and the evil within persons; that there is something in every person that responds to a manifestation of love; and that unmerited suffering inflicted upon one by the enemy is redemptive. All of these assumptions have been questioned and require careful analysis. It is enough here to raise the issue. The love of the enemy is a costly grace.

Finally, the neighbor to be loved is not merely the "next door neighbor." The Good Samaritan story makes this plain. The love of one's people, one's race, or one's class is not adequate to meet the requirements of the Christian faith. The church growth theology that stresses the love of one's own kind is a manifestation of "cheap grace." It would suggest that churches should follow cultural patterns and not meet the challenge of pluralism so characteristic of our time.

The despised Samaritan comes within the purview of Jesus' love ethic. In our day and land, the Samaritan is black, yellow, and brown. Some would say that the Samaritan is a woman. The point is clear: the Samaritan is not our "kind of folk" and yet this is how God loves and this is how God expects us to love one another.

But beyond this, the Good Samaritan story told today must point beyond private ethics to public ethics. How do we express love as we resist racism, sexism, and classism? How do we express love as we join the oppressed in a quest for a just economic order? Love must take us into the arena of collective evil. We must tackle unemployment, we must oppose the Moloch of war. We must seek to avert a nuclear holocaust. It is not sufficient that we take the one who has fallen among thieves to a place of personal healing; we must also seek to make the Jericho road safe for all travelers. Love is a costly grace.

CHAPTER 7

Justice in the Service of Love

There have been a few prophetic individuals in this century who exemplify the theme of this chapter. Martin Luther King, Jr., and Mahatma Gandhi come immediately to mind. They stand out because they knew the meaning of love in the service of justice. Furthermore, their profound ethical understanding of religion, Christian and Hindu, brought psychological and political liberation to millions.

The "social justice" content of religion enabled these persons and others who were moved by the same élan to transform social structures as well as to mediate comfort and assurance to individuals. Our discussion here will first introduce the concept of justice. We will then discuss the relationship between justice and love. Our concluding remarks will take up the theme "Justice in the Service of Love."

Meaning of Justice

Since we are working in Christian theological ethics, let us begin within a biblical context. The Old Testament doctrine of God is based on the idea of justice. The relationship between God and persons was based on the idea of justice. God is the author of justice. A just God is bound to act justly. This assertion is the solid ground for Old Testament faith. It is the common denominator that gives religious unity to Israel: prophets, priests, lawgivers, the common people. All these persons in Israel are convinced of the justice of God as the basis for hope. Yahweh is the foundation of justice from which all Old Testament codes of law are derived. The will of God bears final authority on civil and legal questions. God is the supreme judge, and divine authority is involved in the details of Israel's historical situation.

What has been said applies to human behavior toward both God and humanity. Old Testament writers show a preference for a juridical view of ethical and religious practice. They constantly see the righteous pleading their cause before the judge and winning their case. The righteous are those whom God's verdict has justified, and the wicked are those whom God has condemned. The righteous live by their fidelity: they escape the death penalty planned for them by their enemies through their unflinching faithfulness to God's commandment.[1]

We must look briefly at the Greek contribution to the meaning of justice before turning to the New Testament. Greek society from the eighth through the beginning of the fifth century B.C. was based upon the idea of justice: religious, political, and ethical. The mythical figure of the goddess of justice preceded the logical conception of justice. The virgin justice, the daughter of Zeus, was honored and revered among the gods who dwelt on Mount Olympus. Later, Hesiod turned the figure of the goddess into the reign of law. Justice is a natural quality, a quality independent of human beings but one they cannot evade. Recognition of justice in politics leads to its discovery, by analogy, as the law of the universe. The advance from punishment by an external deity to immanent punitive justice leads to the conception of a divine world order. So it is in Anaximander, Parmenides, and Euripides. Thus, Heraclitus has it, "For the sun will not pass his bounds, else will the avenging deities find him out." In justice all virtue is comprehended. Justice is not merely an inner quality, it is also the legally prescribed behavior of the citizen toward society. When Plato makes the conception of justice the guiding principle both for the state and for the individual in his *Republic,* he refers back to the roots in pre-Socratic thought.

Aristotle devotes an entire book of his treatise on ethics to justice. He gives two meanings to the concept of justice. On one hand, justice is the highest ethical ideal; it is virtue toward another and therefore the chief virtue of the civil life. On the other hand, justice is viewed as the principle that regulates the relationships of people to each other within a community or state; it is both "distributive" and "corrective." This is the restricted sense that the term usually bears in the language of jurisprudence, "to give to each his own." This sense of the word is frequent also in theology, especially the relationship of God and the moral order of the world.[2]

In the New Testament we encounter the notion of righteousness. This term corresponds to the verb meaning "to justify." Paul uses this language sometimes in an ethical sense and again as an equivalent of salvation. When he writes of the law of righteousness (Rom. 9:31), he is referring to ethical demands of the Mosaic law, but when he uses the phrase "righteousness of God," he means that salvation which God accomplishes through Christ (Rom. 3:21). In the Pauline epistles, the word "righteousness" is used in three senses. First, reference is to that ethical conduct which is demanded by Mosaic law; second, it points to the salvation that is the gift of God through Christ; and third, it indicates that ethical conduct which is demanded of the Christian, involving as its minimum turning the other cheek, going the second mile, and humility in the performance of duty (cf. Luke 17:10).

The conception of justice holds a conspicuous place in Christian literature. Its meaning wavers between a more spiritual personal salvific interpretation and a more juridical ethical meaning. In the English language, the legal use of the term "justice" has tended to cloud its use in the Bible as a synonym for "righteousness." This separation is unfortunate, if the "ethical" input is missing in either law or theology. The Stoic conception of justice is noteworthy in its impact upon Christian theological ethics. The influence of Cicero upon Ambrose is a case in point. Ambrose adopts the four cardinal virtues of the Greeks and maintains that the Christian fulfills the ideal of the just person. The cosmopolitan and cosmic ethic of Stoicism is seminal to an ethical foundation for Christian thought and belief. Ethical foundations are deeply embedded in all of creation. The enrichment of the graces of redemption, faith, hope, and love do not uproot the natural virtues of wisdom, temperance, fortitude, and justice. Against this background, Augustine concludes that justice is love serving only the beloved and rightly governing. Aquinas assigns to justice the duties of religion and neighborly love. In both instances, we observe the pronounced "ethical" content of justice in human relationships.

Love and Justice

In Augustine and Anders Nygren, we have profound but contrasting views on love. In essence, we have in Nygren love *without* justice, while in Augustine we encounter love in the service of justice. In the spirit of Bonhoeffer's *Cost of Discipleship*, we have on one account (Nygren) love as *cheap grace*, while in Augustine's love as *caritas* we have the possibility of encountering love as a costly grace.

Augustine includes acquisitiveness as an ingredient in love. Love involves a craving for something that we do not now possess, a quest after happiness, after some good, some *bonum*. All human beings love—it is inherent in finitude. As temporal and dependent beings, they seek goods beyond themselves. The fact that human beings are not self-sufficient explains the desire to reach out in love. This love Augustine conceives as morally neutral—it is neither good nor evil in itself. It is made one or the other by the object toward which it is directed. If the object is able to satisfy our deepest need, the expression of love is good. Conversely, if the object is unable to add anything to our being or offer us any abiding good, the love of it is false and hence evil. We become like that which we seek or love.

There are two kinds of love, according to Augustine—the love of God and the love of the world. The former Augustine called *caritas* and the latter *cupiditas.* The love directed toward the eternal is *caritas,* that directed toward the temporal is *cupiditas.* Augustine's love of God or the quest for the divine is developed under the influence of Plotinus. The Plotinian *eros* is love as the human ascent to god.

In contrast to Augustine, Nygren attempts to define *agapē* as a purely giving love. Love thus understood has nothing to do with desire or craving—it is opposed to *eros.* Nygren clearly observes that the pure Christian conception of love was confused with elements borrowed from the Greek doctrine of *eros* as well as from the Jewish notion of *nomos* ("law"). This process, according to him, reaches its culmination in Augustine. Nygren quotes the New Testament and Luther as authorities in his rejection of Augustinian love.

Nygren argues that Augustine's *caritas* stands opposed to the *agapē* of the New Testament, which teaches that Christian love is primarily God's love. It is a spontaneous and unmotivated love, directed toward God's creatures. Among human beings this love appears in its purity as love for one's neighbor. This love is God's gift to humanity and is itself a purely giving love. It does not consider the merit of its object. Patterned after the divine love, it is directed toward one's enemies as well as toward one's neighbors and friends. God is the ultimate ground of Christian love.

This criticism of Augustine cannot be finally decisive in view of the Augustinian doctrine of grace. Salvation, according to Augustine, involves an ascent to God only by means of divine enabling grace. Saving faith is therefore a gift of God. Divine grace, divine love, is its source. The Augustinian doctrine of predestination is an expression of humankind's dependence upon God for redemption. Salvation is incarnational and the incarnation is the highest expression of divine salvific love. Human love of God and divine love of human beings are essential elements in Christian love.

This issue between Augustine and Nygren comes to clear focus as Christians seek to apply the love ethic in personal and social relationships. The duty to love one's neighbor is derived both from love to God and love to self. Self-love refers to a proper respect for one's personal worth. Contempt for oneself can produce selfishness but not self-love as intended here. In loving others, we do not love them in their present unworthiness; we love the image or likeness of God in them. Love of self as well as love of others is grounded in the love of God. The commandment to love God includes the summons to love one's neighbor. It is the divine image in human beings rather than human beings in their fallen state that we love. The love of self and the love of others point to the highest good, and this can be obtained only by the act of loving God. Love of neighbor is at once a love of God in the neighbor and an attempt to awaken in the neighbor the love of God. As Christians we love ourselves because in doing so we love God. We begin with self-love; and since this in its purity is really the love of God who is in us and in every human being, self-love carries with it the duty of love to others.

If the object of love is totally worthless, we have a sound basis for the human need for grace. But this gracious love may be cheapened by the fact that human beings are robbed of the dignity they have in creation apart from the merits of grace. God, as author of nature, has bestowed worth upon us in the creative act. Sin has marred the image, but it has not been demolished. Moral love must take account of the innate capacity and dignity of the human soul. Love of self and love of neighbor are constituents in the love of God. Along these lines we come to a meeting place between love and justice— a place where justice may be enlisted in the service of love.

The Western theory of justice is derived from two main sources —classical philosophy and Christianity. Aristotle plumbed the depths of the meaning of justice. His reflections upon this concept have influenced jurisprudence and theology down to the present. The Hebrew prophets have had a similar impact upon religion and ethics. In Christian theological ethics, Aristotle's ideas of justice have been blended with the scriptural contribution. This coalescence of the classical and the biblical understanding of justice held together in jurisprudence and theology down to the Age of Reason.

Upon the emergence of the Age of Reason, the law of nature and the law of reason became one. Natural law received a naturalistic interpretation. With the coming of positivism in the philosophy of law, justice lost its metaphysical and supernatural perspectives. A view of justice became relative. Justice was separated from any notion of eternal law, stripped of its divinity and abandoned to the human will. Law was conceived as the product of any reigning power. The way was prepared for the proclamation that any ruling power is supreme. The totalitarian state, as well as the racist state, represents legal positivism in political practice. This happens when justice is no longer viewed as being rooted in the being of God and in the very nature and structure of the universe.

But if justice is rooted in the nature of God, there may be a problem stemming from our understanding of God. If the understanding of God is filled with ethical superlatives, then the perspectives on human behavior and social philosophy will be of high quality. Suppose, however, God's character is misunderstood and God, in fact, becomes the embodiment of gross evil and injustice. The result could be an unjust social order. It is ironical that the endorsement of injustice is almost as apparent in the United States as it is in Iran. The New Right has sprinkled holy water on the American success story. When injustice is supported by religious faith the suffering of the masses makes little impression upon those in power. Throughout human history the rulers who have claimed divine rights have been the most brutal and inhumane. The proper understanding of God is crucial to a proper understanding of justice, for evil and injustice as well as righteousness and justice may prevail in the name of God.

Justice and Love

When one compares the law of retaliation in the Old Testament and the Code of Hammurabi (ca. 2100 B.C.) with the Sermon on the Mount, it would appear that Jesus speaks of love more than justice. In the older materials, justice is based upon exact judgment. Jesus advocates a justice tempered by mercy or justice transformed by love. We observe here a vital relationship between love and justice in the teachings of Jesus. Love without justice can become sentimental, and justice without love is harsh. Justice needs the enrichment and transfiguration of love. Love needs the objectivity and firmness of justice.

Paul Tillich is helpful on this point. He asserts that mutual forgiveness is justice only if it is based upon reuniting love. Christians base this forgiveness upon their experience of justification by grace. Only God can forgive, because in God alone love and justice are completely united. The ethics of forgiveness are rooted in the message of divine forgiveness. Otherwise they are delivered to the ambiguities of justice, oscillating between legalism and sentimentality.[3]

Compare this with the insights of Emil Brunner. Love and justice are radically opposed, according to Brunner. Love is related to persons, never to things. The relationship between love and personality is closer than that between justice and personality. We may appropriately speak of a just law or system, whereas it is improper to speak of a loving law or system. In the personal sphere, therefore, love rather than justice is the highest good. Justice, on the other hand, is concerned with the person in regard to something. Love, according to Brunner, does not ask what is mine or thine; it does not render to the other what is due, what belongs to him "by right," but gives of its own, giving precisely that to which the other has no right.[4]

Brunner wants to maintain the radical difference between love and justice and at the same time hold that they are closely related and derive from the one God. Justice, he insists, is strictly realistic, sober, and rational. Love is a free gift, it is directed to the concrete person in his or her uniqueness. Justice belongs to the world of systems, not to the world of persons. At the same time, all systems are for persons, but never persons for systems, for love knows no systems. Brunner goes on to assert that love begins where justice has already done its work. The demand for justice can be filled; the demand for love can never be filled. Love can fulfill justice but cannot itself be fulfilled. Only love can be perfectly just. Love fulfills all the commandments of justice because it knows that its real work begins only when justice has been done.[5]

Brunner is right in insisting that in some sense love takes us beyond justice. But I am concerned about the dichotomy he sets up. Unless love redeems justice in personal and social relationships, it is difficult to understand how love can make any difference in concrete personal and community situations. When we deal with persons-in-relation, we need to indicate the mutual impact of love and justice under real-life conditions. If both love and justice are moral attributes of the divine personality and if this Being is unitive, it is difficult to understand why these virtues are so far apart in the realm of ethics and concrete human relationships. Brunner has attempted to resolve this dualism on the theoretical plane. We observe his inability theologically to bring love and justice together. He is hampered also because he insists that the only idea of justice is the impersonal manifestation of justice in the form of law. We therefore insist that love and justice not merely "co-exist," they "inexist" in that they are mutually enriching and they reinforce each other in personal and social ethics.

Justice in the Service of Love

Martin Luther King, Jr., in his researches into ethics and theology, found Reinhold Niebuhr's realism refreshing and helpful. King was looking for an ethical perspective that would be useful in his attack upon the systemic evil of racism. He affirmed the realism of Niebuhr while rejecting his pessimism.

According to Niebuhr, love is the basic law. Love is the final structure of freedom. He defines love as *agapē*, the immortal love, the outgoing, unmeasured love of Christ on the cross. Niebuhr's understanding of the relationship between love and justice is suggested in the paradoxical phrase "impossible possibility."[6] He points at once to the ever-present relevance of love in Christian life and to its difficulties. Human beings are finite and sinful and seldom love without self-interest. Christ on the cross reveals love in its perfect form. Here is revealed at the same time God's love and history's meaninglessness, human lovelessness and destructiveness. The Christian ethic cannot be simply love, for human beings live in history, and perfect love is always being crucified in history.

It follows that Niebuhr cannot envisage a society of pure love as long as human beings are true to their nature. Mutual love is possible to some extent, but pure love cannot be a foundation for an adequate social ethic because of human sin. Every definition of justice presupposes sin as a given. Because life is in conflict with life, because of sinful self-interest, we are required to define carefully those expressions of justice which prevent one life from taking advantage of another. A responsible approach to social problems concerns itself with structures of justice that may help to equalize power. Love can never be a perfect alternative to the "pushing and shoving" that characterize justice. Niebuhr is a realist who acknowledges at once the possibilities and the injustice inherent in sinful humanity. He opposes sentimentalism, irresponsibility, and false hopes in human possibilities in history. But Niebuhr is not a defeatist. He is aware of the almost unlimited potential of human beings who are capable of self-transcendence. It is unfair to use his "impossible possibility" in the cause of inertia or quietism. His ethic of realism clearly enlists justice in the service of love. He brings a concrete and sober perspective to an otherwise abstract and sentimental discussion.

George Thomas has made the significant observation that there is a difference between the ideal and the actual as far as social justice is concerned.[7] But he insists that insofar as the ideal is realized in actual systems of justice, there is no dualism between the requirements of justice and those of love. Justice, in fact, becomes an indispensable expression and instrument of love. The distinction between the ideal of justice and love is simply that justice establishes the general conditions for the good life of a group and represents the demands of love for all persons of the group. Love at the same time seeks to fulfill the special needs of persons, individually and in relation to other persons. Love requires the criticism and transformation of actual justice according to the goal of ideal justice. Since the actual justice of every society in history falls short of the law of love which provides the perspective for this criticism, the process must be continuous.

Albert Knudson goes a step farther and insists that justice is implied in love. Love is not independent of justice and does not exist without it. Knudson asserts that if we interpret justice in relation to the rights of others, it is simply the other side of love. If, on the other hand, by justice we understand retribution or requittal, it is a constituent element in Christian love. Without love, justice would lose its moral character. What gives love its superiority over justice is its personal warmth and intimacy, its positive goodwill and redemptive role.[8]

Conclusion

When we desire to enlist justice in the service of love, there must be a dynamic mutual relationship between them. In the theological ethics of Augustine, there is between love and justice what Robin George Collingwood calls a "distinction with a difference." But at points between them, there is a difference without a distinction. In Augustine's blending of the Greek classical virtues with the Christian theological graces, the cardinal virtues—wisdom, temperance, fortitude, and justice—are adopted as full heirs by Christian theology upon the condition that they be baptized. Love, as in Pauline thought, is the more excellent way—it is the Christian grace par excellence. But justice also encounters the biblical understanding of righteousness. The sinfulness of human beings is brought face-to-face with the saving grace of God. Between love and justice there is a difference not merely of degree but of kind—that is a distinction with a difference. Yet when love transforms and Christianizes justice, it not only supplements justice quantitatively but it enriches justice qualitatively. Justice, being thus transformed, becomes love serving only the beloved and therefore rightly governing.

The manner in which justice and love interpenetrate each other on the plane of concrete personal and social relationships may in some way transcend human language as well as thought. But on the level of human experience when the struggles of life must be engaged, there is abundant evidence that justice serves the purpose of love and that love exalts justice to a higher level.[9] There are biblical, theological, and ethical resources to undergird this affirmation.

It is essential that this affirmation be more than a belief held by individual Christians. The churches as institutions need to enlist justice in the service of love. Sinful social structures must be opposed by structures of righteousness if the evils of the system are to be overcome. We have the assurance that the Lord of the church is self-giving love. A statement from the Oxford Ecumenical Conference of 1949 provides a convenient summary of this statement of justice in the service of love. It reads as follows:

> The proclamation of the gospel of Jesus Christ includes in itself responsible utterances on the direction which ought to be followed by positive law among men. What the Church has to say on the subject of human law and justice cannot remain isolated and in separation from its proclamation of the crucified, risen and returning Lord.[10]

CHAPTER 8

The Power to Be Human

This chapter focuses upon the place of power in Christian theological ethics. A theology of social justice has been around a long time, but liberation and political theologies have lifted up in a unique way the issue of power as it relates to love and justice. Black theology grew out of the affirmation of black power. Priest-theologians in Latin America forged a theology out of the faith that the "resources of grace" are available to break the power of evil. Political theology in Europe is the result of the constructive Christian dialogue with Marxists. Feminine theology is the result of a sharpened consciousness of women who oppose sexism. What all these theological movements have in common is a thirst for liberation and a concern for the humane use of power.

As one who was nurtured in an otherworldly piety, I much appreciate the positive aspects of these new approaches to the doing of theology. Salvation has been viewed in this tradition as primarily personal salvation. It was often negative and legalistic. Vital religion is more than a dike against hell or a passport to heaven. It is more than sentimentality also. Christian theological ethics must deal with tough decisions and the reality of power but in a way that makes life more human.

The Meaning of Power in Christian Theological Ethics

When we observe close up our human condition, the evils we often overlook that are extremely destructive to us are structural. While we may not be as repentant of personal sins as we should be, these do get the most attention in our moral preachments. We must in no way abandon an intense concern for personal sin and salvation. We are becoming aware, however, that sinful social structures often destroy persons, families, and communities. Their effects reach into our most intimate relationships. To eradicate evil we must address collectivities—we must confront "principalities and powers."

A proper theological understanding of power and its humane use is at the heart of a just social order. Without humanizing power, love is "cheap grace." Power is a crucial concept as Christians confront secular structures. In times like these when power is so wantonly abused, it seems unholy to dare to suggest that Christians get involved in politics. Yet the political order together with the economic order determines the survival of our very life. With the quality of life bound up with the political economy, it is difficult not to get involved, if only as victim. For example, we are facing a reduction in the human services at the same time that our tax dollars are feeding the Moloch of war.

The mixing of religion and politics has now become the order of things in an overt manner. When sermons were preached in the White House, we had an undisclosed mixing of religion and politics. Now we have an open and blatant involvement of fundamentalist ministers in political affairs. This creates much confusion in the minds of many believers. It also presents a peculiar challenge to black church leaders who have been involved politically on behalf of their people from the inception of Afro-American history. The issues are joined. What is the nature of the God we believe in? Which cause is just? How can Christians profess faith in the same God, belong to the same denomination, and yet interpret the will of God in such a conflictual manner?

Religionists who formerly fought against any involvement of Christians in politics have now jumped in on the side of injustice and inhumanity. They believe they speak infallibly for the God of common worship. This is not the same situation that Martin Luther King, Jr., faced. When he wrote his "Letter from the Birmingham Jail" he had the task of convincing his white and Jewish colleagues that they should get involved in the struggle for racial justice. He attempted to persuade them that it was their Christian duty to oppose unjust law. He argued that it was essential to their devotion to God that they participate in the liberation of fellow human beings.

We face, as we have previously noted, a new breed of politicized evangelists who have joined the political establishment on the side of the privileged and against the suffering masses. These religionists seek to sanctify the present order. They believe that power and privilege come to those who are divinely blessed. Our theological task now is that of desacralizing an unjust order that is in power. The question is no longer whether faith leads to involvement. It is, rather, how that faith can inform us and empower us to usher in a

more just and human order. Are there resources of grace flowing
from the Christian faith which will transform this society for the
ends of love, justice, and humanity for all people? To pose this
question is to raise the theological issue of the nature of *power*. We
are forced by circumstances to deal with the moral issues associated
with the mature use and abuse of power.

Power is deeply rooted in the Judeo-Christian understanding of
God. God is often viewed as being omnipotent, almighty—the ultimate source of power. Various divine activities are explained by the
attribute of power. The all-power of God is understood as a manifestation of God through revelation. It is assured, however, that
God enters into self-limitation in order to share power with human
beings and in order to grant us freedom of selfhood and the responsibility of persons.

God exercises power in creation and in reconciliation. Creation
is a manifestation of God's almightiness. In divine loving and judg-
ing we observe evidence of God's power. Power is the means
through which God achieves a holy purpose in creation, redemption, and sanctification.

God is said to hold sovereignty over creation and history.
Through a powerful providential direction, God takes charge of
human and worldly affairs. God's absolute power is self-limited only
by virture of the balance in the divine nature between ability and
ethical integrity. Because all power is inherent in the character of
a God who will do right, we must oppose any idolatry of power
within history and creation. God is sovereign power. There can be
no divine rights of earthly rulers. All human power is under God's
judgment. Paul, in observing that government is ordained of God,
should have distinguished between what God permits and what God
ordains. The sovereignty of God excludes the absolute power of the
state and of the people. All human power is limited by divine power
and eternal law.

A theology of power in Christian perspective must acknowledge
the primacy of the power of God and at the same time categorically
reject the absolutizing of any form of human power. The Christian
still owes ultimate allegiance to God. Under God all earthly rulers
and communities stand in constant judgment. This God of power
is one who loves and cares for all. God is especially concerned for
the deliverance of the oppressed from all forms of human bondage.

God shares power with human beings. Moral power in the service
of justice and love is available. Because there is a source of power
for us through grace, we are able to cooperate with God in the cause
of social justice. Power to be good is a divine gift for us. Power itself
is morally neutral. It may be used to create or to destroy, depending

upon the purpose for which it is employed. Power, like freedom, can be exercised to curse or to bless. We are invested with power to hate or to love, to do good or to do evil. We have the power to be free or to enslave ourselves or others. The proper use of power under God is for good ends—for freedom, justice, and righteousness.

The affirmation that God has the ability to realize the highest moral ends is critical for faith. It sustains a believing trust in a God who is able to keep promises. It is important especially for the oppressed to have the assurance that God is the only absolute source of power. Such a belief is essential in order to hope in the midst of the absence of power over one's life. To know a life of poverty, to be subject to abuse as a black or as a woman, as a child or as an old person, is to know life without power and without hope. It is also to be aware of the awesome power of sin and evil, both personally and collectively. This power of evil must be broken. When there is a power of evil, there must be a greater power for good if the victims of the evil power are to be set free.

We need to know that justice and love in God are sustained by power. God's love will prevail because divine power is unchallenged ultimately by any contrary power. God is the Lord of history and will have the last word. We know that it is better to trust God than it is to put confidence in human beings. The moral nature of God and the almighty power that sustains the divine purpose are on the side of love and justice. Power supports but does not supplant love and justice in God.

The Coalition of Love, Justice, and Power

Even though Bultmann held that the motivation of love must be in the will rather than the emotions, it was Tillich who sought to pull love, justice, and power together in a dynamic way. We will trace briefly his discussion that led up to this coalescence.

Tillich asserts that without the *eros* toward truth, theology would be impossible, and without *eros* toward the beautiful, no ritual expressions would exist. Without *eros* toward God, love is replaced by obedience to God. Obedience, however, is not love. It can even be the opposite of love. *Eros* and *philia* go hand in hand. While *eros* represents the transpersonal pole, *philia* represents the personal pole. Neither of them is possible without the other. One who cannot relate oneself as an "I" to a "thou" cannot relate to the true and the good and to the ground of being in which they are rooted. In *agapē*, ultimate reality manifests itself and transforms life and love. *Agapē* is love cutting into love, just as revelation is reason cutting into reason and the Word of God cutting into all words. The ulti-

mate basis for the Christian's life and action is *agapē*. *Agapē* seeks the
other in his or her center and sees other persons as they are seen
by God. This is the line of reasoning that leads Tillich to conclude
that foundational love is rooted in the will. According to Tillich,
there is something at the basis of love that justifies its ethical and
ontological interpretation. Love is the drive toward the unity of the
separated. Love manifests itself most where it overcomes the greatest separation.[1]

It is but a step from this ethical and ontological understanding of
love to the coalescence of love with justice and power. Once love
is conceived in terms of a motivator of the will and power that unites
those who are separated, the availability of power for love to accom-
plish its task is to be assumed. Again Tillich speaks in glowing terms
about the ground and power of being as a basis for all of his assumptions in both theology and ethics.

Why not affirm that God is a being with a well-rounded character?
The divine creator, redeemer, and judge has as attributes of character love, justice, and power, among other qualitative characteristics.
Let's assume at the same time that God represents not only the
embodiment of the highest ethical ideals that are manifested in the
divine relationships to the nonhuman sphere of creation; that these
divine ethical superlatives are even more pronounced in the divine-
human encounter; and that the divine being has the *ability* or the
power to make goodness and rightness come to pass in history and
providence. A divine being who creates, sustains, and redeems
human life inspires in us a believing trust precisely because there is
an interrelationship between love, justice, and power in our understanding. The Author of nature, the Lord of history, and the Giver
of grace are ways of referring to God as creator, providential sus-
tainer, and redeemer. The attribute of power is just as essential to
the divine nature and activity as are love and justice.

Again as we look at the incarnation, we are moved by the manner
in which love, justice, and power coalesce. There is the identification of the Revealer of God's salvific purpose with the lowliest. Jesus
is born in a stable, he is wrapped in a blanket used for sick cattle,
he is from Nazareth, his associates are social outcasts—even his
death is between two thieves. The method of his death is cursed by
the Jews and ignoble to the Romans. Yet shepherds welcome his
birth, the blind receive sight, the deaf hear, the lame walk, the poor
hang on his words, and the disinherited become his close disciples.
The cross demonstrates the profundity of God's love. It also illustrates the critical confrontation of good and evil on the plane of
history. It is through the resurrection that we get to know the triumph over evil and death. It is this event of Christian history that

inspires us to struggle for what is just and right. It is the Pauline Christ mysticism which makes this existential in our understanding. When we are "crucified with Christ" and "share his resurrection" power, then we absorb in our own experience the meaning of this message at the heart of Christian life.

Where there is sin, there is grace in our personal life. We have been loved and we are to express this love in our personal and social relationships. It is when we confront "the principalities and powers" of this world that we often have difficulty translating this message of love into ethical decisions and actions. We may be moral individuals and extremely "immoral" in the social context. This is not always because we have evil intentions. Sometimes we have a limited or narrow understanding of the gospel. Sometimes our limited vision leads to implicit support of unrighteous causes of which we are not even aware. Someone has well said that the only thing necessary for evil to succeed is for good persons to do nothing. When we attack sin and evil on all levels the coalescence of love, justice, and power becomes inherent in all that we are as Christians.

The Power to Be Human and the Humane Use of Power

Both Reinhold Niebuhr and Martin Luther King, Jr., have an understanding of power—King more in relation to love and Niebuhr more in relation to justice.

King addressed "the blatant abuse of white power" and the emergence of "black power" on the eve of his death. He does some critical analysis of "power" itself which deserves careful attention. King observed that American power is unequally distributed. Blacks have sought their goal through love and moral suasion devoid of power. Whites, on the other hand, have sought their goals through power devoid of love and conscience. He saw this as a conflict of immoral power with powerless morality. King viewed this as a major crisis of our time.

Power for King was the ability to achieve purpose. It is required to bring about social, political, and economic changes. Power is desirable and necessary to implement the demands of love and justice. Love and power are not polar opposites. Love is not the resignation of power and power is not the denial of love. In King's view, power without love is reckless and abusive and love without power is sentimental and anemic. Power, then, is love implementing the demands of justice. Justice, at its best, is love correcting everything that stands against love. With these understandings, King was prepared to assert that black power can be creative and positive. In this sense, the call for black power is a call to black people to assess the political and economic strength to achieve their legitimate goals. Power is essential for the struggle for justice. It is obvious that King was reaching out to the new black movement. He sought a means to absorb its best insights without abandoning the love ethic and the way of nonviolence.[2]

In some way Niebuhr's strong view of justice and his unusual insight into the stubborn character of structural evils serve as a corrective to King's emphasis upon the primacy of love expressed through nonviolent means. Niebuhr's *Moral Man and Immoral Society* deserves a second look in this regard.[3] King saw love as the absolute norm of human behavior and the ultimate goal of human society. Niebuhr, on the other hand, saw justice as the final goal, with love as the ethical judge of every approximation of justice.

Niebuhr's belief in the prevalence of the egoistic impulse in every person led him to emphasize the need for a realistic understanding of the abuses and uses of power. He saw relationships between social groups as basically political, not ethical. Social relations, he believed, are determined more by how much power each group possesses than by the moral claims of each group. In other words, the issue in most social conflicts is the possession or lack of power. Social inequity is the result, not of the failure of religious and rational people to act more lovingly and reasonably, but the possession of an inordinate amount of power by a particular social group or class. The concentration of power in one social group leads to the entrenchment of power, and power automatically gives that group a privileged position and an advantage over other groups.[4]

Privileged classes always resist change because they are beneficiaries of social injustices. Power continues to exploit weaknesses until it is challenged by countervailing power. Social groups with power, property, and privilege do not voluntarily relinquish any of these advantages; on the contrary, advantages have to be wrestled from them. The dispossessed have a higher moral right to challenge their oppressors than these have to maintain their status by force.[5]

Like Martin Luther King, Jr., James Cone and other black theologians have had to deal with the evils of power and powerlessness. Insofar as all liberation theologies, whether Latin American, Asian, African, black, feminist, or otherwise, have had to speak for the liberation of the oppressed (the powerless), they have had to encounter the meaning, the use, and the abuse of power. Niebuhr anticipated our concerns realistically insofar as the difficulty of this matter of collective power is concerned. While Niebuhr appears to have been too pessimistic, the Marxist may well be too optimistic. Some liberation theologians may be overly optimistic as well. We must balance a sense of the radical depths of sin and evil, both personal and social, with a strong emphasis upon the grace and power of God.

Let us note Niebuhr's understanding of the meaning of power as well as the relationship between love and justice. Sin has a radical meaning in Niebuhr's thought. Justice is therefore the highest approximation of love that finite persons can achieve in social institutions and structures. The ethical goal is not love but justice. When measured by the norm of love, every system of justice is imperfect, and every social program is a compromise. It then becomes appropriate to talk in terms of the balance of power.

Without this balance of power the most loving relationships may degenerate into an unjust state. Love is the fulfillment of justice in the sense that love serves to expand the potential of justice. Love is the negation of justice in that love transcends justice. Love provides an absolute standard by which to judge both personal and social righteousness.[6]

We may ask how this balance of power is to be obtained and how it works in the oppressed-oppressor relationship. A minority in power does not willingly balance power. Niebuhr is realistic here also. He indicates that the power of the oppressor must be interrupted. The weakness of the oppressive system must be found in order to topple the entire system of oppression. When this interruption occurs, power is diverted and the once "relatively" powerless have power. We must never assume the absolute powerlessness of a people.[7]

Niebuhr's views are instructive in comparison to King's views on power.

It is significant that King began to criticize Booker T. Washington, while he found the more radical W. E. B. Du Bois praiseworthy. King observed that Washington underestimated the structures of evil. Washington's philosophy of "pressureless persuasion" only encouraged white racists to become more ruthless in their oppression of blacks. Du Bois, King noted, was concerned with the use of coercive power to relieve oppression and to achieve liberation and social justice for all people.[8]

Thus King toward the end of his life seemed to see more clearly the stubborness of entrenched power structures. He saw that the oppressed cannot achieve their rights without confrontation and constant pressure upon the social groups in which power is concentrated. King was painfully aware that those in power would not give up their advantages without strong resistance. He urged blacks to identify levers of power and grasp these controls in order to influence the course of events.

We have no conclusive evidence regarding where King would

have gone with his philosophy and movement if he had lived. There is every indication that he would have intensified his efforts. He had organized a coalition of poor people with the intention of paralyzing operations in Washington. But his call to Memphis to aid striking garbage workers ended his life and career.

King made a powerful witness, and it is for those of us who have survived his death to carry forth the task. We must look at events that have surfaced since King's death to be responsible in judgment and action. Without a critical analysis of our social, economic, and political situation, we cannot meet the challenge of the hour. Our understanding of racism, as well as other forms of inhumanity, must be set in the context of the geopolitical realities of the world community. Only thus may we speak meaningfully about love, justice, and the humane use of power.

Power requires careful direction. It must be used to serve love and to fulfill justice. We are advocating a humane use of power. Power is to be used to realize the highest human values: personal, social, and institutional.

CHAPTER 9

Faith in God
Confronts Collective Evils

The problem of evil in a world created by a good God is not a new issue. It is as old as the human mind's reflection on ultimate things. The word "theodicy" has been used to name this problem in philosophy and theology. The problem of evil and God has often been discussed from a conceptual, mainly a metaphysical point of view. It has usually involved ethical questions, but these issues have centered in theoretical concerns. I wish to approach the problem from the vantage point of undeserved human suffering. While I do not discount pain and suffering from other causes, my objective here is to confront forthrightly the existence of suffering based upon inhumanity. What accountability does God have, as creator, in the suffering that human beings inflict upon each other? This issue arises for theists—it does not necessarily occur to humanists. If human beings are on their own, then the culpability of the divine in human suffering need not arise. But if God is a creator and provident God, the question is inescapable.

It would appear that a limited number of Euro-American theologians have just discovered what Jürgen Moltmann calls the "crimes of history." Previously they had mainly viewed sin and evil in very personal terms or as natural evils. But the death camps of Hitler's Germany raised to a level of visibility a problem that had been ignored. The same issues are involved in any consideration of slavery or colonialism. And we should not overlook sexism and poverty. The issue of human suffering on a grand scale is with us in the United States, Central America, the Middle East, and especially in South Africa today. But the pacesetters in Western theology have generally overlooked this crucial theme.

A number of theological programs now approach the question of suffering as a political, sociological, and economic concern. The issue of suffering is no longer confined to the realm of the personal and psychological aspects of faith. Political theology, liberation the-

ology, holocaust theology, black theology, and some African and
Asian theologies, all seek to develop a theological perspective that
takes seriously group suffering and systemic evils. But as powerful
as this company of thinkers may be, the ecclesiological and theological mainstream seems almost ambivalent to the cries of the oppressed. This places an undue burden upon the few theologians
who seek to think theologically in solidarity with the suffering
masses. This task is, however, so important and urgent that those
who are involved do not have the luxury of awaiting approval by
respectable theologians in the American mainstream.

As the oppressed seek to eke out a survival, theologians as well
as church leaders seem to be obsessed with fine points of doctrine
and ideological differences that have little to do with making life
more human. With many in positions of political and spiritual leadership calling this nation to move in a direction that promises even
more widespread human suffering, denominations are preoccupied
with the divinity of Christ, the inerrancy of Scripture, and creation
versus evolution. The American national administration appeals to
the well-off and flirts with military solutions to human problems.

Our discussion will focus upon the area where there is human
responsibility related to free moral agency. The reason why human
beings are responsible and free is a theological problem of some
moment. Could not God have made human beings unresponsible
and unfree, morally speaking? Doesn't God possess the power to
contradict logic and ethics as understood by finite minds?

To suggest such a possibility about God makes us uncomfortable.
But to transcend logic and ethics does not and should not necessarily require contradiction. We have a sense that God embodies the
best that we know as finite persons and yet baffles our ability to
comprehend fully. In other words, we may know in part, but we do
know. We see through a glass darkly, but we do see. Theology
should direct us to the place where faith possesses reasonableness
and certitude even if certainty is not within our grasp.

Our concern for the alienation caused by human suffering should
not lead us to question the moral integrity of the very source of the
faith to overcome suffering. There needs to be an understanding of
human suffering and of God that strengthens confidence in the One
worthy of trust.[1]

Human Suffering and Pain

Pain is inevitable as a part of our creaturely existence. Human
beings experience what we may describe as "animal pain," because

they live in a physical body in a natural environment. The physical world is often harsh—it is indifferent to the moral or spiritual state of human beings. The fact that we dwell in a natural environment, usually governed by law, means that the violation of a physical law leads directly to painful consequences. Violation of natural law may be due to ignorance as well as to willful acts. Every infraction of natural law is met instantly with swift and exacting penalty. There is no "grace" or "mercy" in nature. It is accurate to recall that nature is "red in tooth and claw." There is a "thingness" about nature. Animal pain is unrelated to the moral and spiritual quest.

Furthermore, there are times when the cosmos seems to become a violent chaos. Earthquakes, tornadoes, floods, and diseases are examples. Human beings are victims of what seems to be the anger, even the wrath, of nature bereft of its usual order. Those who happen to be at the wrong place at the wrong time are destroyed without exception.

Natural evils are difficult to understand and even more difficult to accept. Even though we may have logical and scientific explanations for many natural events, we have a tendency to ascribe moral interpretations to such experiences of "animal pain."

The question of moral evil immediately raises the issue of responsibility. Christians have a sharpened problem because they dare to believe in a Creator-God who is said to be all-good and all-powerful. Furthermore, God is assumed to have created the world "out of nothing." Where, then, does evil come from? There is no preexistent "stuff" as in Plato's *Timaeus,* no Plotinian "matter" or Hindu "maya." God is said to have created the world and described it as good.

Belief in the goodness of creation complicates the argument that sin as moral evil results from the wrong choice. The question of source, of choice between good and evil, baffles our minds and tests our faith. Some Christians who are aware only of personal sin attempt to account for the origin of sin and evil in the transgression of Adam and Eve, which they define in purely sexual terms. This is too simple an answer to such a complex issue. It is clear that sin and evil involve more than the abuse of sex in personal life. But when we take a look at sinful social structures we are overwhelmed by the complexity of evil. Greed is a deadly sin that is at least as perverse as lust. Yet greed, like lust, is more effect than cause. The question From whence comes evil? remains an intellectual puzzle. For instance, the "moral majority" would eradicate sins associated with *lust,* but they are "the silent majority" when it comes to *greed.* We need to take a careful look again at what medieval theology referred to as the seven deadly sins. It might help to look at the Ten Commandments and the Sermon on the Mount with some social sins in mind.

As we look at human suffering, resulting from inhumanity, greed causes as much havoc in public ethics as lust does in personal ethics. In the case of pimping and prostitution, *lust* and *greed* reinforce each other. Marital infidelity usually illustrates lust more than greed, though they are often combined. But it is possible for a person to be a paragon of virtue in faithfulness to family ideals and values and yet be the perpetrator of great misery for thousands of human beings through economic exploitation. In fact, this sponsorship of widespread suffering of other races, individuals, and families may be carried out for the sake of an enriched family life. For the sake of the comfort of one's own family, one may be an agent of destruction of other families, not because of lust but because of greed. I would not place a greater or lesser value on these deadly sins, but I wish to make the point that in the realm of ethics, there are no easy answers. There are only hard questions. We do, however, have principles that direct us forward.[2]

Evil and God

The question of Job is, Why do the righteous suffer? The existence of human freedom as bestowed by God has been one of the classical Christian responses to the reality of evil and undeserved suffering. I use the word "response" here, because I am not aware of any definitive "answer" to Job's question. The "free will defense" (of God's justice and love) does not explain all moral evil, and it would appear not to touch natural evil. The Christian response that seems to be most helpful is a faith response. It centers around God's redemptive work in Christ. The Easter story, rightly understood, enables us to engage evil and suffering, transmute it for constructive ends, and move forward in hope to God's future and ours.

We dare to believe that God is a creator spirit and that God is a benevolent provider. Our trust in the meaning of life is supported by a faith in a supreme person who is the source of all that is loving and just. But not only do we believe that God is good, we believe that there is sufficient ability in God's being to sustain the best ideals and values we know in history and human experience.[3]

There is no logical way out of the dilemma that God is both all-good and all-powerful. One attribute reinforces the other. Both are essential for a well-balanced divine personality. We believe this in spite of the widespread existence and persistence of sin and evil.

If God is all-good and *will not* put an end to moral evil, we have a problem. If God is anxious to eradicate evil and *cannot*, whence divine omnipotence? Both the desire to have goodness triumph and the ability to bring that triumph to pass are the twin affirmations of theistic faith.

If there is a logical answer to this mystery, it is only the logic of faith. Christians have found their faith solution in the cross and resurrection of Jesus. Evil is not explained logically, it is transmuted spiritually. It is faced and it is conquered. The experiential answer is the sufficiency of God's grace to enable and sanctify. The manifestation of grace works in and through us. Just as much suffering is caused by the abuse of freedom, much healing can flow from God's grace working through that same freedom. Human beings can be agents of good as well as evil.

Co-Creators and Co-Laborers

Though we cannot account for the origin of evil, we are painfully aware of its radical nature and destructive power in personal and social relationships. Much of the evil, resulting in mass suffering, can be attributed to the abuse of freedom. In the face of knowledge and freedom to choose and act nobly, we deliberately choose a lesser good. Collective evils are more difficult to explain and to overcome. We find moral individuals in an immoral society. The task of analyzing sinful social structures is awesome. Consequences of sins and evils may be passed on in the context of history and the social environment. How do we place guilt and responsibility and find the means to overcome such evils?

Much moral evil can be explained through God's self-limitation in order to create beings who are both free and morally responsible. Much suffering is present in our personal and social lives because of the perversion of our nature. Freedom is abused and we have not been responsive or responsible as co-creators with God. We are endowed to scale angelic heights, but we have sunk to diabolical depths. Much of the answer we seek is in the recovery of the creative purpose of human life in the design of God.

The Need for Liberation

In *A Tale of Two Cities*, Charles Dickens speaks of "the best of times" and "the worst of times." Our cities, our nation, and indeed the world is a tale of two cities: black and white, males and females, rich and poor. Viewed from the perspective of Christian faith, times of great adversity may be our finest hour of commitment to the values and goals that matter most. Our faith in God is a resource that enables us to make creative use of suffering.

I have walked the streets of Calcutta. The horsemen of the Apocalypse roam freely around the streets of that city. But I would not have the deep compassion I feel for people in Calcutta unless I identified with the plight of the black poor in the cities of America.

Sometime ago, as I drove a daughter to Spelman College, we stopped at a drugstore. It was the day when government checks were being deposited. On one side of the street was a bank. Diagonally across the street from the bank was a drugstore. We observed the large number of elderly persons who filled the streets, sidewalks, stores, and banks. I had just left my own parents in North Carolina and along the way I had spent some time in Washington. The plight of the black, elderly poor occupied my thoughts. Beyond the sheer compassion I felt, I pondered the effects that the conservative, national, political regime has upon the plight of the elderly. I asked myself who will bind up these wounds.

A little later on that same day a young woman, an acquaintance of my family, called me. This young woman, though black, has become a highly successful model in New York City. She indicated that she was visiting a friend at Atlanta University Center and would like to have lunch with me. In a prelunch conversation in my office, to my surprise she described her success with complete detail and abandon. At twenty-four she seemed to feel that she was entitled to all of this. She did not know that her success outstripped her achievement of more basic goals, that natural beauty fades, and that this is often a long life. And then I was even more startled when she said, in a tone of voice that anticipated my approval: "God gives me everything I ask for!" I was tempted to put on the mantle of a preacher or prophet and expose the deficiencies of her God of success. But I realized that she needed her God, even though too small. She moves daily in a world of human exploitation where her best friends are often sophisticated call girls. Her upbringing and her religious faith have brought comfort and direction to her life. A devastating confrontation would not have helped. Therefore I found a way to remind her that others who are equally devout are not as successful as she has been in the affairs of this world. In a subtle way I encouraged her to seek a deeper understanding of God and God's ways of dealing with us human beings.

As we look around our cities, we have great evidence of prosperity: large hotels, skyscrapers, and church edifices of great magnificence. There is a climate of progress, expansion in many areas of life. But concurrent with all this affluence is unemployment, hunger, poor housing—grasping poverty. Many people in our midst live from day to day on the edge of survival. It is not sufficient that we contrast this with deprivation in some Third World country. What we see in cities throughout the United States is poverty in the midst of plenty. We are talking about Lazarus receiving, as it were, the crumbs from Dives's table.

I am concerned about our inhumanity in relation to persons who are black, poor, female, or aged in all towns and cities in this country.[4] We are haunted by the results of our national sins. Racism and poverty are the Trojan horses within the walls of our cities. Our greatest dangers are within our own nation. If there were no crises abroad, we would still be in trouble. Our internal national sins of racism and greed are the seeds for our own destruction.[5]

We must be concerned about police brutality. In the *Atlanta Constitution* a twenty-three-year-old black man was shown being beaten by a white police officer while two other officers held him. In Los Angeles a black woman, Eula Love, was killed with many shots from police in the presence of her small children. The matter would have gone unnoticed if the black ministers and their followers had not decided that we have had enough. The Gathering, made up of hundreds of black ministers in Los Angeles, had become a powerful force for monitoring these situations.

Our prison system is crowded with young, black, intelligent, and often gifted men and women. We not only warehouse our aged, we are doing the same with our youth—especially black, poor youth. This systematic incarceration and dehumanization of generation after generation of black males impacts upon black women and children. The perpetuation of this situation replenishes the reservoir of the candidates for a life of crime, violence, and imprisonment. Spiraling welfare rolls, juvenile delinquency, illegitimacy, pimping, prostitution, dope addiction, and alcoholism are among the inevitable consequences of this vicious cycle assured by racism —America's national sin.

The time has come for us to break this circle of deprivation with programs for social transformation. We must consider what racism does to the psyche of black people. It triggers self-hatred and dislike for those who look like us; for we are often guided by the distorted image of blacks in the white mind. How else can we explain the high incidence of homicide among young black males? At the same time, racism produces a superior self-image in whites. Even poor whites exalt themselves above the most affluent and successful blacks. Racism is a cancerous growth in America. It is tearing our nation apart.

Attempts to Find Solutions

One-Dimensional Religion

For some Christians, personal salvation is the solution to everything. This is undergirded by a sentimental Jesusology and biblical inerrancy. There is nothing wrong with spiritual formation, the deepening of the inner life, or a radical personal conversion. But this answer is inadequate, because the conception of both sin and salvation is limited. The trouble with the simple view of the gospel is that it is unaware or ill-equipped to deal with the difficult questions that human beings face in this world.

This type of gospel can easily become demonic when it is preached to people who are undergoing gross suffering, deprivation, and injustice. If one is privileged, this gospel can also serve diabolical ends. When the Christian God is understood as the author of success and pride of race, religion becomes destructive both to its advocates and to its victims.

Religion can also be one-dimensional in a this-worldly form. This form is difficult to distinguish from secular humanism. Human beings consider themselves self-sufficient. One seeks to bring in an ideal order without dealing with human sinfulness (both personal and corporate) and one cuts off the relationship with God. Where there is no sense of sin, there is no need for the forgiving grace and power of God.

In some sense the tragedy of Jonestown with the appeal to have-nots and the victims of racial injustices illustrates what happens when human beings put their intimate trust in an earthly "messiah." A young woman who declared, "My mother died at Jonestown," described how her mother was transformed from a saintly to an obscene person in that movement.

The Church Growth Thesis

This approach builds upon the American success story. In the name of Christian love, its advocates believe that the most loving thing to do is to establish homogeneous unit churches where each race, class, and ethnic group will worship and fellowship among its own kind of people.

This movement would abolish efforts to create interracial congregations. It would not attempt to bring Spanish-speaking people into the fellowship in English-speaking churches. This approach asserts that the easiest, most natural manner of dealing with our human relations problems is the most Christian. It ignores social justice issues and the need for unity in diversity in the body of Christ. This cannot be the appropriate response to the sins of racism and greed in a pluralistic society.

The Moral Majority

What had been a few years ago a "silent majority" has become a self-defined "moral majority." A few years ago black church persons were assailed because they dared to advocate the moral and social implications of the gospel. Now we are told that the gospel is literally defined in the American traditional way of life. Free enterprise, competition in business, democracy, and the work ethic are taken directly from inerrant Scripture. There is, however, a remarkable silence regarding racism, greed, and all social, economic, and political injustices. The limitations and one-sidedness of their interpretations are apparent. The exposure of this gospel through their mass media presentations should give all of us real concern. How shall we counter this multimillion-dollar brainwashing of the very people who need to know the gospel as *liberation?* Their answers are too simple because they have not dealt seriously with the question.

The International Perspective

We live in a global village. Technology and economic factors have made it so. Interdependence has made us one in destiny. Racism at home and militarism abroad will not save America.

There is a relationship between exports and imports and our national economy. The connection between the importing of cars from Japan and the near-collapse of the automobile industry is apparent. We need to compare an almost zero unemployment rate in some countries with unemployment in Detroit. This reality is very destructive of the black and poor people who are the last hired and first fired.

There is a relationship between the amorality of transnational corporations as they control the economy of poor nations and many problems here at home. These financial giants defy the sanctions of governments against them. Their lobbyists are so powerful that they are able to have their way regardless of the concerns of politicians and preachers alike.

A neo-colonialism, in psychological and economic forms, is practiced in the Third World. Many peoples in our world still have an inferiority complex vis-à-vis Western peoples. The inferiority-superiority complex of colonialism is aggravated by the persistent power of racism at home and abroad. Many Christian denominations are still building their missionary movements upon the sinking sands of racism and colonialism. With the rising tide of liberation consciousness, time is running out. But many minds still need to be decolonized.

Again, we are deeply involved in the economic exploitation of traditional peoples in the Third World. We have enlisted our economic resources in support of the rich and powerful few against the weak and suffering masses. South Africa is a real test for capitalism and democracy. Their racism and colonialism are still alive and well. Our banks, businesses, and even our churches are under the judgment of God in South Africa.

There is a close relationship between our situation at home and our image abroad. We have not learned that our "big stick" diplomacy does not and cannot work. Here too we have "a tale of two cities." The two-thirds world is uncomfortably nonwhite, poor, and non-Christian. There is a strong sense of fellow feeling between the have-nots on planet earth. We do not have sufficient wealth or military power to prevail in a world where two thirds of the human family are against us.

National Pride/Human Rights

Reinhold Niebuhr, a prophet-theologian, wrote of America's pride of race, pride of wealth, and pride of power. Unless we are able to do away with these prides, they will become the Trojan horses within our gates—and we will self-destruct. There still remains the real ideological military and socioeconomic challenge of Marxism. Our only hope is to make our way of life more humane.

Under the Carter administration there was much talk about human rights. There is some real question about the practice of human rights—especially at home. A case in point: Why did not President Carter use the moral influence of his office to resolve the unjust decision against the Wilmington 10? Was he a victim of the common fallacy of trying to do abroad what needs to be done first at home?

There is a strange phenomenon among Christians. Some Christian bodies are very much concerned about world hunger, but they show little if any concern about hunger on their doorsteps. At a planning session on global solidarity in theological education, it was reported that a certain seminary had built their program of study around world hunger. They felt they had solved the problem of international theological education. But after spending several months at this seminary, I found they were doing little about addressing human relations problems on their campus, in the city where they are located, or in their state. How could they become a model for an international program of theological education?

Our approach to human rights must be broader than the Christian covenant. It must be interfaith, interreligious, interethnic, and intercultural. It must be based upon mutual respect for the equal dignity of people, something like the cosmopolitanism of the Stoics which influenced the development of the natural law–natural rights tradition in the West. Our dignity must now be inherent in our humanity. This affirmation could be undergirded by the ethics from the great religions, but not dependent upon them for its validity. According to our confession, Christians should lead the way.

Conclusion

There is no easy or final answer to the theodicy question, but each Christian has to live with it and no serious theologian can bypass it. I have my own provisional perspectives. My faith is grounded in the God who raised Jesus from the dead.

Since human beings are free and responsible and much mass suffering stems from human sins, such as racism, greed, and sexism, I place heavy emphasis upon human beings as co-workers with God for the triumph of goodness in the world. It follows that much attention must be given to the process of placing the gospel into the social context of both national and international problems. As faith in God confronts collective evils and mass human suffering, we human beings, especially Christians, work as fellow sufferers and co-laborers with God for beneficent ends.

CHAPTER 10

Black Theology in Dialogue: Two Examples

Thus far we have discussed black theology as a serious dialogue partner with political, contextual, and liberation theologies. In this chapter we shall examine the relationship of black theology to two other theologies. Minjung theology, now developing in South Korea, is cultural and historical but essentially *political.*[1] In this chapter we attempt to explore the lines along which a fruitful dialogue may take place between black and Minjung theologies. The focus of the reflections on Jewish liberation theology has political expectations, but the strongest affinity between Jewish and black theologies would appear to be how faith has enabled both communities to translate the memory of suffering into a vessel of hope.

I. COMMON THEMES:
BLACK THEOLOGY AND MINJUNG THEOLOGY

We will explore some common themes in two theological traditions in what may generally be designated as "liberation theologies." To so identify them may be confusing, but Latin American liberation theology cannot be considered as normative for this worldwide movement, except in a representative sense. It would appear that black theology has more in common with Minjung theology than it has with some other options in liberation theology, such as the Latin American program.

Black theology itself is not monolithic. Black theology is based upon the black religious experience, culture, and church tradition. It is a unity in diversity. Black theologians differ in the manner in which they conceive a common tradition, and their intellectual and spiritual journeys are varied. For example, Howard Thurman and Martin Luther King, Jr., are both black theologians who did their work out of the heritage lifted up by the latest group of so-called black theologians. While much of the latter thought is based upon "a political model," some of the earlier work was *ethical* but *cultural* as well. Black theology should be broadly conceived, including a strong emphasis upon history and culture, without toning down the essential liberation thrust.

This more comprehensive view, which balances cultural and political interests, has the advantage of a strong outreach in reference to both African and Asian theological developments. For example, the political model relates directly to the South African situation, but as Mbiti reminds us, it does not have the same strong affinity with most of Africa which is postcolonial. A cultural affinity does exist with all of Africa, however, yet this does not get adequate attention in all black theology programs. Here we will use this more comprehensive view which will provide a more serious response to Minjung theology.

Reflection on Roots

Let us consider the similarities in history and culture that inform black theology and Minjung theology.

The situation giving rise to black theology has been given serious attention in the United States by several religious and secular scholars for almost twenty years. It is not necessary to chronicle this history here. A brief review is all that we will attempt. (I have provided my perspectives on this history in chapters 2 and 3 of this book.)

Black theology arose out of an upsurge of black consciousness and black power in the late 1960s. It was a combined search for cultural roots and the power or means of liberation from racist oppression. It continued "the stride toward freedom" of the Martin Luther King, Jr., project. The new movement had both continuity and discontinuity with the work of King. In fact, it was the culmination of more than three centuries of struggle.

A similar foundation can be laid for the emergence of Minjung theology in the Korean setting. Korea has been caught between the great Asian powers for many centuries. It has been in the crossfire of conflicts between such powers as Russia, China, and Japan. This has led to much suffering on the part of the Korean people. In more recent times, Korea was a colony of Japan; then, following World War II, it was divided into North Korea and South Korea. The invasion of South Korea by Communist North Korea led to a tragic war, involving the United States as well as other nations. In the period since that tragedy, South Korea has witnessed several oppressive governments. Even today it is in a real sense a security state, with frequent infringements upon human rights. The masses of Korean people have been victimized by these crucial historical realities. They have had to search for meaning and seek survival under these repressive circumstances.

This history of suffering has run parallel with the Christian missionary movement. First the Roman Catholic Church established itself in Korea. This was followed by the Protestant missionary effort which has been present in Korea for about a century. Because of the Korean experience of so much mass suffering from political oppression, the gospel took on a prophetic as well as a priestly interpretation from its introduction in Korea. This seems especially true of Protestant missions.

Christian efforts therefore, in both the Korean and the black theological developments, have non-Western foundations. Blacks are Afro-Americans. Black theology affirms African roots. Minjung theology is built upon pre-Christian religious, ethical, and cultural factors. Apart from traditional African cultural and religious traits, it is not possible to have an in-depth understanding of black theology or the black church, family, or cultural tradition. Confucianism, Buddhism, Shamanism, and other elements are likewise essential to the Korean context. These are related to the development of Minjung theology. Finally, there is a holism in the African and Asian worldviews that may account for a real affinity between blacks and Koreans in their way of developing theological thought. For example, in both cases there is a ready acceptance of the exodus paradigm in doing theology.

Response to Oppression: People as Subjects of History

One of the most difficult actions for a people victimized by a situation of oppression is to find a constructive nonviolent response and resistance. It is easier to resort to fatalism or violent revolution than it is to formulate a plan for massive resistance against structural evil through nonviolent means. This is why the work of Martin Luther King, Jr., has such worldwide significance. Even though the method was introduced by Gandhi, it was given its classic expression in the Christian love ethic by King.

The need for an active response to oppression has been underscored by David Shanon, a black biblical scholar and educator. He strongly emphasized the need for Afro-Americans to become "subjects" rather than "objects" of history. Persons who have been victimized and handicapped by a long history of oppression, whether blacks, Hispanics, native Americans, women, or the aged, will be defeated by circumstances unless they take their destinies into their own hands. While this expectation is difficult when one has suffered a depletion of material resources and psychological resources as well, it does seem to be an essential posture for the underclasses in American society.

Some blacks have resigned themselves to what they consider the fate of alienation and suffering. Rampant unemployment has led to alcohol and drug abuse and all types of personal and familial tragedies. Others have turned to the solace of religion. Emotional and otherworldly aspects of religion have provided compensation for those who are denied the fulfillment of life here and now. On the other hand, from the resources of religion there have emerged advocates of social justice who have given black people the courage to claim their dignity and struggle for freedom in spite of the hopelessness of the real world in which they live. Religious faith can provide "resources of grace" that enable people who are by circumstances "objects" of history the means to become "subjects" of history. This is in essence what the "exodus" theme in black religious history is all about.

This concern to become subjects rather than objects of history has been evident in many parts of the world. It was especially prevalent in countries moving from colonialism into periods of nationalism, development, and liberation. The writings of Frantz Fanon are noteworthy in this regard. Paulo Freire's writings on consciousness-raising have been celebrated not only in Latin America but worldwide. A people who internalize their desire to be free are not easily enslaved. A former GI who fought in Vietnam reflected upon his experience. He observed that from the first engagement with the Viet Cong, he knew they were likely to win the war because of their determination. They were programmed psychologically and ideologically not to be defeated. When a people change from being objects of history to subjects of their history, they become a force to reckon with. Then they are motivated from within and are prepared to confront whatever odds they must face in the quest for liberation.

Like black Americans, the Korean people compare their experience with that of the Israelites of the Bible. So much of their history seems to parallel that of the people of the Old Testament. Korea has been the battleground of the great nations of the Far East. Its people have suffered because of power struggles between the great nations. The theme of the exodus and the message of the prophets of social justice help to define their reality. They see God as acting in their history as in the Old Testament period.

In this regard there is a similarity between the experience of Afro-Americans and Koreans in the manner in which they have appropriated the message of the Bible as they have understood their experience. In both cases the leadership style of Moses and the theme of the exodus have been freighted with great meaning of freedom from oppression. The slave songs, especially the spirituals, and Korean music, dance, and drama have taken up this message in a powerful way.

The Meaning of the Cross

Because of the common experience of suffering, black theology and Minjung theology focus strongly upon the meaning of suffering. Theodicy is a controlling category. The problem of structural evil and the consequence of mass suffering is inescapable. This reality can be met with resignation as well as skepticism or it can be translated into a source of strength.

Recent black theologians as well as Minjung theologians, upon contextualizing the experience of suffering, have elected to engage it. They not only accept it as a given but they seek to transmute it into a source of moral and spiritual resistance to evil. They do not attempt this out of defiance as some existentialists such as Albert Camus have done. Neither do they accept the "humano-centric" approach of William Jones in *Is God a White Racist?* But they adopt a Christocentric model, for the most part. In both cases the Jesus of history is also the Christ of faith.

In developing an approach to evil and suffering, they are moved to reexamine their Christology. Minjung theologians have examined the message of Jesus to the poor. They have sought a deep understanding of the Jesus of history and the secular meaning of the gospel. Bonhoeffer's writings have been very helpful as a backdrop to much reflection on the life of Jesus and the meaning of his cross.

Concurrently, black theologians have sought after the Jesus of the "disinherited." The adoption of the symbol of the "black Messiah" has surfaced as a way of dealing with the self-identity crisis and the situation of racism and poverty. There has been an examination of traditional Christological models, but with a view to how these may speak more forcefully to the reality of black suffering based on the experience of continuous oppression. Again this has led to a serious engagement with the cross of Christ.

In black and Minjung theological programs there is a reluctance to dwell upon the regal or kingly role of Jesus. The stress upon the resurrection does not overshadow the weight given to the cross of

Christ. The lordship of Jesus so easily undergirds a situation of domination of the weak by the powerful. Emphasis upon the resurrection easily points to otherworldliness and triumphalism to the disadvantage of any oppressed group. In black and Minjung theologies the emphasis upon Jesus' cross leads to a balanced view of the resurrection. There is no resurrection without a cross. The regal role of Jesus is brought into a dynamic relationship with his priestly and prophetic ministry.

A Christological model that is either otherworldly or only regal is generally acceptable to a repressive order. It does not challenge the established order which is in violation of human rights for the mass of humanity suffering from oppressions such as poverty and racism. It does not speak redemptively to the underclass. The tendency, therefore, is for the privileged class to enthrone a regal Christ as the sanctifier of the status quo. Those who see Christ as the liberator are likely to be subject to denunciation and persecution by those in power. This is why black as well as Minjung theologians have chosen a different dimension of Christology in which the cross is central. But the cross is not a symbol of escape; rather, it is a symbol of engagement with evil and suffering. Christ's victorious resurrection is seen in relation to the cross as its sequel and ultimate vindication.

Conclusion

This brief excursion into comparative theology is highly suggestive of the rich possibilities toward human understanding that could result from vigorous activity on this theological frontier. In a comparison of black and Minjung theologies we note important differences, but there are significant similarities between them.

There are a cluster of factors in both backgrounds that are similar and that result in a holistic ethicoreligious outlook. When we translate this into biblical terms, it leads to a view that blends social justice concerns with the healing dimensions of the gospel. In both instances the exodus theme points to the message of the prophets of the Old Testament who denounced oppression and advocated justice as well as mercy. Again, both black and Minjung theologies seek to find the historical Jesus and the secular meaning of the gospel for human liberation. This in no way dilutes the meaning and power associated with the cross-resurrection event. The Christ of faith is Lord, but he is also liberator. In these and other ways black and Minjung theologies may open new doors to cross-cultural understanding and the ecumenical dialogue and mission of the church of Jesus Christ.

II. BETWEEN MEMORY AND HOPE:
THE PILGRIMAGE OF JEWS AND BLACKS

The time is long overdue for theological conversation between blacks and Jews.[2] We share a common concern for liberation from oppression. In both cases the exodus has had great meaning. Our common reflections should lead to a mutual depth of enrichment.

In American history, Jews and blacks have shared each other's pain and have worked together toward the solution of human ills. More recently, however, through historical events and through a rash of unfortunate statements, alienation has surfaced to endanger this understanding and cooperation between the two peoples. If Jews and blacks are to continue to work together, they will need to understand in a profound way each other's religion, history, and outlook. We need to go beyond our common experience of oppression and share the more positive affinities in our heritages as well.

The Remembrance of Things Past

Jewish people have a legacy of anguish and struggle. They have experienced wanderings and lament. Their contributions to spiritual depth as well as to the prophetic critique of injustice have been profound. A special emphasis has been placed upon God's providential purpose in human life and history. It is surprising that we had not heard more from Jewish theologians regarding the interpretation of history in the light of faith in this time of liberation.

With the emergence of liberation as a seminal theme, Marc Ellis points to the experience of bondage and freedom as a significant paradigm. Implicit in his reflections is the experience of exile as indicative of an event with liberation content. Exodus and exile have surfaced often in other forms of liberation theology as symbolic ways of describing oppression, and Ellis takes us back to the history of the very people whose religious history gave rise to these symbols of faith and meaning.

The immediate occasion for the use of these ancient symbols was the Jewish experience of the Holocaust. The Holocaust refers to the death of six million Jews under Hitler in World War II. It represents an attempt at ethnic genocide of the Jewish people. Behind the Holocaust is the event of the exodus as a point of reference. The exodus speaks to all who seek to know the meaning of suffering. It symbolizes both struggle and hope, both bondage and freedom. Ellis sees this dialectic of slavery and liberation as being at the heart of Jewish life and history, and each generation is to think through this message anew.

Any student of black history finds it instructive to read Jewish history, especially in reference to the experience of ethnic suffering. The exodus is the exegetical thread that runs through black religious history from its inception to contemporary black theology and that has provided the perspective for preaching, music, and thought. The remembrance of things past in reference to bondage and freedom is a sacred thread that provides continuity for the faith of black Christians. It follows that the call to remember the providential purpose of God in the liberation of Israel of old has profound meaning for black people no less than for the providential purpose of God in the liberation of Jewish people. Blacks participate in this event indirectly through the revelation of faith rather than through their direct participation in the exodus or the Holocaust. Slavery in the United States provides the paradigmatic connection to the exodus in the history of black faith.

Liberation Theologies: Jewish and Black

Ellis has presented a cluster of reflections by diverse Jewish thinkers on the Holocaust. Black theologians in recent years have similarly looked at suffering in black history in search of meaning.

Ellis has described the contributions to this quest for meaning of Elie Wiesel, Richard Rubenstein, Emil Fackenheim, and Irving Greenberg. Wiesel sees some value in keeping the memory of suffering alive. Rubenstein advocates human solidarity in a desacralized world. Fackenheim sees Jewish suffering as a testimony to the possibility of survival in an age on the edge of extinction. And Greenberg asserts that after Auschwitz we can speak only of "moments of faith"—that is, faith between periods of doubt.

From the black perspective, an important aspect of this discussion is the issue Greenberg raises about the role of Christians as persecutors of the Jewish people. This has been a constant concern of black theologians. Christianity as a religion seems to be easily domesticated. In great crises like black slavery or the Holocaust, churches too often seek self-preservation rather than accept the moral challenge of the time. I agree with Ellis that Christians have not come to grips with the difficulties of faith raised by the Holocaust, but neither have the churches faced the implications of slavery and racial discrimination. It is not too difficult for black theologians to understand the significance of this for their future. Not only is there silence on these matters but there is also indifference. This explains the anemic condition of much Christian confession.

It is significant that theodicy has been a constant theme through black religious literature, including the oral tradition. Sermons, poetry, music, folklore, and formal theology all raise questions regarding the meaning of undeserved suffering. Among the recent black theologians, William Jones has suggested that theodicy should be the controlling category. While other black theologians have not been that explicit, it is unlikely that one could read a major text of a black theologian that does not touch on this issue. There is therefore a real affinity between black and Jewish theologies of liberation on this common theme. We should be able to learn much from each other.

From Memory to Hope

As Jews attempt to derive meaning from their past experience of suffering, they find themselves on the periphery of sociopolitical and religious consciousness. They find themselves in solidarity with others who are suffering under the dominant economic and political systems of our time.

Ellis points to four movements that are addressing the following formative events of our time: the Holocaust, the birth of Israel, and the direction of Jewish life. The following are noted: (1) a neo-orthodox movement led by the charismatic Arthur Waskow; (2) the New Jewish Agenda, a community of progressive religious and secular Jews; (3) the Religious Zionists for Strength and Peace; and (4) Jewish feminists. These several movements appear to address internal problems in the Jewish community while developing solidarity with the oppressed outside their ranks.

The struggle of the Jewish community and its quest for meaning and identity have much in common with the black consciousness movement in the United States, and the theological insights resulting also share commonalities. The more balanced black theological positions have provided vigorous internal criticism while reaching out to join other victims of oppression in their struggles for liberation. This is the only way to a common hope.

The discussion of Ellis on the dialectic of empire and community is very instructive. Empire, he asserts, seeks to create structures to control the weak. Community, on the other hand, advocates equality and cooperation. In some ways Jews are ahead of blacks in acquiring success and empowerment through existing power structures. They are therefore former victims who, forgetting their past experience of suffering, could easily make victims of other peoples —for example, blacks in the United States and Palestinians in Israel. But affluent blacks are not far behind them in this tendency. Allowing the weak to enter the existing structures of domination does not assure the humanization of those structures.

History reminds us that Christians as well as Jews can easily lapse into idolatry and serve oppressive structures, thus making new victims. The worship of power and materialism are the major sins of the modern world. According to Ellis, Jews who learn from their heritage of the exodus have the experience to overcome these things. The recently acquired idols of capitalism, nationalism, and survival are obstacles to their sense of purpose. The bridge between religious and secular Jews, however, may depend more upon what it means to be human than upon belief in God. Israeli militarism and expansionist Zionism must be critiqued, according to Ellis. And North American Jews need to address neo-conservative support of unjust power as well as the power of global American capitalism. America as a land of freedom and opportunity for Jews is at the same time an empire that imprisons the will and distorts values as the cost for affluence and power.

The neo-conservative black leadership in several agencies in Washington makes us aware that the danger of being co-opted and forgetting the plight of the weak exists for all peoples. Hence, the warning that Ellis aims at his Jewish colleagues is applicable, especially at this time, to blacks as well. Jews and blacks live between memory and hope. Our watchwords are: "Lest we forget!"

Conclusion

In this chapter black theology has become a dialogue partner with Minjung theology in South Korea and with Jewish liberation theology in the United States. What we are pointing to here is the kind of dialogue that John Cobb has expressed as he has brought process theology into conversation with political theology and Buddhist theology. Cobb dares to speak of "crossing over" and "returning" to one's position, having experienced a type of "transformation" in so doing. Where there is this intensity in our efforts at a two-way conversation, there is the assurance that new light will break forth on both sides of the discussion. Black theology faces the need to dialogue with other theological partners for the sake of others in sharing, but equally as much for its own sake in receiving. In this process of maturing, dialogue is one indication that black theology has now come of age.

CHAPTER 11

The Future
of Black Theology

A theology in context is not necessarily relativistic. It does not mean that each person or each people will go their own way without regard to what others believe and think. Contextual theology is mindful of what others think and believe.[1] It reaches outward at the same time that it reaches inward. Dialogue has been used extensively in the present reflections because it is essential to the outlook we espouse. But contextualization does require a thorough examination of one's own situation in life as the basis for meaningful dialogue. Our final discussion will be concerned with what seems to be an unfinished agenda of black theology. The indefinite article "an" is used, for there are others who rightly perceive a different agenda or different aspects of a similar agenda. Their concerns are needed as well. Our collective wisdom is essential to the future of black theology.

An Unfinished Agenda for Dialogue

Many of the topics introduced in this study deserve extensive expansion. First, the dialogue between African and Afro-American theologies has just begun. The recent developments in Africa, especially the new concern for hunger and apartheid, have accented the pan-African connection between American blacks and Africans in their living worlds. The factors of race and history solidify this bond even more. Much more needs to be written about similarities and differences between Africans and Africans as well as between Africans and Afro-Americans. Theological developments will reflect this new interest and knowledge.

Second, at the heart of biblical and theological scholarship we have noted a contribution that liberation theologians have made to Christology and ecclesiology. Black theology has a vital part to play in enriching and deepening the understanding of Jesus Christ and the church for all of theology. It is true that feminist theology[2] and Latin American liberation theology can make a similar contribution. Jewish theology and Korean Minjung theology suggest the almost limitless knowledge and enrichment in the "doing of theology" that is possible as we move back and forth from context to dialogue.

Finally, there is the recognition of what contextualization can mean in understanding and overcoming structural evils. Richard Rubenstein has analyzed and chronicled better than most of his contemporaries the tremendous torture, injustice, and sheer inhumanity that human beings have meted out to each other in the twentieth century.[3] So much of our brutality throughout history has resulted from religious belief, even faulty theology, that we need to give serious attention to corrective reflections in this field. Again, we have often seen theodicy in purely personal terms. Liberation theologians rightly expand this to include collective evil and group suffering. We need an interpretation of the faith that treats holistically this critical theme of all theology. Adequate attention has not yet been given to how collective evils increase the personal suffering of the victims of oppression and how faith in God enables these people to find meaning at a survival level.

An Unfinished Agenda for Praxis

The matters mentioned above are more in the nature of tasks requiring theological explication. The concerns in this section are more in the nature of praxis. In keeping with the action-reflection outlook of liberation theologies, serious theological thought is to be given to these matters as well.

First, there needs to be a close relationship between theology and ministry. After some twenty years of the development of black theology, black denominations, pastors, and congregations are not greatly moved by the insights of black theology or black theologians. A way needs to be found to change this. There is no way fully to estimate the value of black theological reflection to the life of black Christians, to the ministry and witness of black churches. Black theology has been not only a faith response but a thoughtful engagement with the souls of black people. It not only aids in assessing the signs of the times, it is deeply anchored in the roots of black culture, history, and church tradition. It has much to offer to black people toward self-understanding and social transformation action.

Since black theologians are knowledgeable and committed, it will be their task to reach out to the churches. It is not likely that there will be aggressive movement in the opposite direction. Black theologians and church leaders started out together in the late 1960s, but somewhere along the way we moved apart. African church leadership and the theologians are much closer than Afro-American ministers and theologians. Often the same person is both a church leader and a theologian. Bishop Desmond Tutu is but one prime example. This need of a theology for ministry should be at the top of the agenda for black theology because so much depends upon the effective ministry of black churches.

Second, black theology must address the fact of poverty in the black community. The economic plight of black people is critical and growing worse. It is on this front that we can profit from liberation theologies dealing with classism and sexism. Blackness and poverty often are inseparable. This becomes increasingly so as affirmative action programs are phased out in favor of individual opportunity. The "color-blind" society that President Reagan talks about does not exist in the United States. Racism is a reality and it is related to the lack of economic opportunity among minorities. Then, closely associated with this, is the "feminization" of poverty which strikes a mortal blow at black single-parent female-headed households with a disproportionate number of dependent children. These situations are intergenerational and lead into a future of despair and hopelessness.

Whatever we are able to do to turn this situation around in a constructive direction will depend upon black people themselves, and especially black churches. Black people will need to embrace values that will make them inner-directed. They will need to become subjects of their history rather than objects. They will need to use good business sense and pool their economic resources for racial uplift. Great potential exists in leadership and economic resources, but the will and the means to realize these ends must be found. Black theology as a theological ethic must engage this problem. Black theology must get involved in social analysis, value clarification, and strategies leading to concerted economic development designed to improve the plight of black people in this life.

The economic power of the black church together with its political strengths could make a difference. Black ministers have successfully rallied black voters. There is still, however, a need for more votes and more knowledge of how the political process works. We need to be more aware of the way in which political power depends upon economic means. We need, also, to be involved in social transformation as well as social service. In sum, we need to be alert to how the social, economic, and political interests of black people hang together.

Black theology is essentially a liberation theology concerned with praxis. Our life in Christ, together with our worship and life-style, as individuals and as a people, should focus upon the improvement of our economic situation. Black theology is holistic—it does not see the well-being of the soul as unrelated to life in the body. Salvation includes the whole person and all of life. Sin and salvation are both personal and social. Evil and suffering are structural as well as personal. Against the background of such an understanding of the gospel, we must deal with the economic factor. Here is an essential contact point of black theology and ministry in the black church.

Finally, black theology must relate to the educative process.[4] Education in all its aspects is the arena of our concern. Black theology is academic as well as religious in its program. It has been in touch with the search for roots in our colleges and universities. Black theologians have examined the findings of historians, sociologists, political scientists, psychologists, physicians, and attorneys. Fine arts—that is, art, drama, and music—have been reviewed. Black theologians have looked carefully at literature as well. Black theology was born in the midst of an intellectual ferment as well as a social upheaval. On the theological front, black theology has engaged contemporary theologies all over the globe. In centers of education, however, there have been inadequate exchanges with other scholars and we have not had the kind of dialogue with our colleagues in other academic fields which makes for enrichment and fulfillment.

The involvement of black theology in the educative process should begin with Christian education in the local churches and should move through the denominational and ecumenical agencies of our churches. It should reach not only children and youth, it should reach adults. In higher education, black theology as well as the study of black religion should be taught and discussed as a staple in courses in black studies, religious studies, and cross-cultural studies. Without an understanding of the spirituality and protest content of black religious experience and the black church—its religious, social, and psychological messages—one does not have an in-depth understanding of black people. A great deal will depend upon black theologians concerning *how* and *when* this is done. They will need to work with sensitive colleagues in the right places to enrich all education for all people.

Theological education presents a special challenge to black theology. Since most seminaries have a majority leadership of white males, both black theology and feminist theology do not usually fare well. Since Latin American theology is often considered to be Marxist, it may even be banned from offerings by conservative Protestant

as well as some Roman Catholic seminaries. Yet all of these liberation theologies are important for those who would engage construc-
tively in a ministry to people in our time. All of these theologies have
a contribution to make to all persons who study them. They should
be considered essential for those who will lead congregations today
and tomorrow.

During these last decades of the twentieth century, the United
States is becoming a Third World nation because of the large
numbers of new immigrants from nonwhite societies and the patterns of natural growth within immigrant communities. A theological education that emphasizes "a homogeneous ministry" or
"ministering to one's own kind" does not speak to the realities of
the church in our world today. Ministry is going to require a cross-
cultural or multicultural ministry in order to be effective. Just as
theology will need to be contextual and pluralistic, even so our
ministry will need to be the same. In the preparation for effective
ministry today, a traditional program of theological education may
not be adequate. It now prepares ministers to deal with personal
and interpersonal concerns, but it does not usually prepare persons to engage social and, even more serious, structural concerns.
In view of the importance of ethical and social issues, Christian
ethics often does not have a prominent place in theological studies. The ethicist is expected to be outspoken on moral questions,
but there is a general feeling that no one needs to take him or her
seriously. In my judgment, black theology, together with other liberation theologies, can have a transformative effect on theological
education. These theologies should be supplementary to traditional theologies but necessary to prepare seminarians for effective ministry.

The Next Steps

We should not be overcome by the difficulties we face in doing
black theology or by its lack of acceptance thus far. It is a task worth
doing, it has great importance for the life of the church, and it is
extremely rewarding for those involved in it. Black theology has
reached a state of maturity as a form of theological discourse. It is
now possible to present its basic content to a wider audience and
in a more far-reaching manner. It is the responsibility of black
theologians to communicate to youth and laity the reflections they
have shared hitherto mainly with colleagues within the circles of
theologians and religious scholars. We must not gainsay the value
of sharing what we have thought and what we believe to our fellow

ministers who will find what we have to share useful in their ministries.

The first step should be an evaluation of what has been accomplished. This book has been an attempt in this direction. But our full assessment may require a more careful statement for critical examination.

Once we have evaluated the past development and the influence of black theology to date, we need to take a second step. We have worked mainly as *individuals*. The dimensions of the task will, I believe, suggest a *team* effort. Black theology, by its very nature, requires knowledge and experience beyond what is possible for any one person. We now have several persons with outstanding ability in a number of theological disciplines. Some of these persons have specialties that bridge nonreligious fields. In our ranks are men and women, Protestants and Roman Catholics. The time has come for us to team up to share our collective knowledge, experience, and resources for a more effective project. This would lead to greater outreach and strengthen our witness.

Finally, very closely related to the team approach of doing black theology is the need to encourage and support each other in our individual work. The life and work of a black theologian can be lonely and thankless. There will always be a place for the creative thinker in solitude. We, as all other theologians, have a personal intellectual and spiritual pilgrimage. Thus apart from our teamwork we must find space for our personal projects. But we will also need to share and publish the results of our private scholarship. Thus we will need to encourage and support each other. As this is done there will be a mutual strengthening and a more effective outreach of our collective project. Systematic theologians need input from biblical theologians. We need to be in touch with church historians, ethicists, and others. The needs are mutual and the rewards could be great. Evaluation, teamwork, and mutual encouragement and support are the next steps forward in black theology.

Conclusion

It is clear that the task of doing black theology lies more in the future than in the past. This book began by defining the contextual method for our purpose. Next we provided the historical background for our study in our history. This also led us to a brief dialogue with African theology today. The heart of the book is both a theological and an ethical account of how black theology engages the critical issues of our time. We then enter again into dialogue with Jewish and Korean Minjung theologies. Once black theology reaches an in-depth self-understanding, it does contribute significantly to cross-cultural theological understanding. The final chapter charts in outline our future task. In a real sense, the end of this volume is but a fruitful beginning. To the future belong our challenge and our hope.

Notes

Chapter 1: Contextualization in Theology: A Discourse on Method

1. The work by Diogenes Allen provides strong support for this observation. See Diogenes Allen, *Philosophy for Understanding Theology* (Atlanta: John Knox Press, 1985).

2. See John B. Cobb, Jr., *Beyond Dialogue: Toward a Mutual Transformation of Christianity and Buddhism* (Philadelphia: Fortress Press, 1982). Here he has attempted to make Mahayana Buddhists (Zen and Pure Land Buddhists of Japan) serious discussants with process theology.

3. Paul Tillich, *Christianity and the Encounter of the World Religions* (New York: Columbia University Press, 1963).

4. See Virginia Fabella and Sergio Torres, eds., *Doing Theology in a Divided World* (Maryknoll, N.Y.: Orbis Books, 1985).

Chapter 2: African Roots of Black Theology

1. J. Omosade Awolalu, "Sin and Its Removal in African Traditional Religion," *Journal of the American Academy of Religion*, vol. 44, no. 2 (1976), p. 275. Hereafter cited as *JAAR*.

2. Ibid.

3. See a review by Gyekye of Mbiti's *African Religions and Philosophy* (Garden City, N.Y.: Doubleday & Co., 1970). The review is found in *Second Order: The African Journal of Philosophy*, vol. 4, no. 1 (January 1975), pp. 86–94.

4. Ibid., p. 91.

5. *JAAR*, vol. 44, no. 2, pp. 275–287.

6. See Aylward Shorter, *African Christian Theology: Adaptation or Incarnation?* (Maryknoll, N.Y.: Orbis Books, 1977), pp. 34–36.

7. John Bennett, "Fitting the Liberation Theme Into Our Theological Agenda," *Christianity and Crisis*, July 18, 1977, p. 168.

8. See Charles B. Copher, "The Black Man in the Biblical World," *Journal of the Interdenominational Theological Center*, vol. 1, no. 2 (Spring 1974), pp. 7–16. Hereafter cited as *JITC*. Cf. Robert A. Bennett, Jr., "Africa and the Biblical Period," *Harvard Theological Review*, vol. 64, no. 4 (October 1971), pp. 483–500.

9. Thomas Hoyt, Jr., "The Biblical Tradition of the Poor and Martin Luther King, Jr.," *JITC*, vol. 4, no. 2 (Spring 1977), pp. 12–32.

10. Ibid., p. 32. Cf. Frederick Herzog, "Liberation Hermeneutic as Ideology Critique," *Interpretation*, vol. 28, no. 4 (October 1974), pp. 387–403.

Chapter 3: An Afro-American/African Theological Dialogue

1. See *Scottish Journal of Theology*, vol. 29, no. 2 (1976), pp. 159–175.

2. James J. Gardiner and J. Deotis Roberts, eds., *Quest for a Black Theology* (Philadelphia: Pilgrim Press, 1971).

3. Kwesi A. Dickson, "Towards a Theologica Africa," in Mark E. Glasswell and Edward W. Fasholé-Luke, eds., *New Testament Christianity for Africa and the World* (London: SPCK, 1974), pp. 199–207. Cf. J. W. Z. Kurewa, "The Meaning of African Theology," in *Journal of Theology for Southern Africa*, no. 11 (July 1975), pp. 32–42. Hereafter cited as *JTSA*.

4. Kwesi A. Dickson and Paul Ellingworth, *Biblical Revelation and African Beliefs* (London: Lutterworth Press, 1969).

5. *Interpretation*, vol. 28, no. 4 (1974), pp. 422–440.

6. *Theology Today*, vol. 27, no. 4 (1971), pp. 422–433.

7. *JITC*, vol. 4, no. 2 (Spring 1977), pp. 12–32.

8. Ellewaha E. Mshana, "The Challenge of Black Theology and African Theology," *Africa Theological Journal*, no. 5 (1972), p. 22.

9. Lecture presented to the Faculty of Theology at the University of Tübingen, October 11, 1977.

10. See Peter Bolink, "God in Traditional African Religion," *JTSA*, no. 5 (December 1973), pp. 19–28. Cf. James H. Cone, *God of the Oppressed* (New York: Seabury Press, 1975).

11. Gabriel M. Settiloane, "Confessing Christ Today, From One African Perspective: Man and Community," *JTSA*, no. 11 (July 1975), p. 31.

12. Ibid., p. 33.

13. Edward W. Fasholé-Luke, "Ancestor Veneration and the Communion of Saints," in Glasswell and Fasholé-Luke, eds., *New Testament Christianity for Africa and the World*, p. 214.

Chapter 4: Jesus and His Church

1. J. Deotis Roberts, *Roots of a Black Future: Family and Church* (Philadelphia: Westminster Press, 1980).

2. Howard Thurman, "a scholar par excellence," wrote an unusual treatment of the life and compassion of the earthly Jesus at a time when most pacesetters would have ruled his insights out of court. But the Jesus that Thurman wrote about is very much like the Jesus of recent black theology and many other liberation theologians as well.

3. Howard Thurman, *Jesus and the Disinherited* (Richmond, Ind.: Friends United Press, 1981; first published in 1949 by Abingdon Press), ch. 1.

4. Rosemary Ruether, *To Change the World: Christology and Cultural Criticism* (New York: Crossroad Publishing Co., 1985), p. 19.

5. See Leonardo Boff, *Jesus Christ Liberator: A Critical Christology for Our Time* (Maryknoll, N.Y.: Orbis Books, 1978); Jon Sobrino, *Christology at the Crossroads: A Latin American Approach* (Maryknoll, N.Y.: Orbis Books, 1978); and José Miranda, *Being and the Messiah: The Message of St. John* (Maryknoll, N.Y.: Orbis Books, 1977).

6. Boff, *Jesus Christ Liberator* p. 285.

7. John D. Godsey has provided an excellent theological exposition of this work in his *The Theology of Dietrich Bonhoeffer* (Philadelphia: Westminster Press, 1960), pp. 27–55.

8. John W. DeGruchy, *Bonhoeffer and South Africa: Theology in Dialogue* (Grand Rapids: Wm. B. Eerdmans Publishing Co., 1984). It is generally observed that Bonhoeffer was greatly influenced by black spirituals and the black church tradition during his first visit to Union Theological Seminary in New York. See Godsey, *The Theology of Dietrich Bonhoeffer*, p. 24.

9. John Yoder, *The Politics of Jesus* (Grand Rapids: Wm. B. Eerdmans Publishing Co., 1972), pp. 34–35.

10. Ibid., pp. 147–150.

11. See King's *The Measure of a Man* (Philadelphia: United Church Press, 1968), pp. 39–59.

12. Avery Dulles, *Models of the Church* (Garden City, N.Y.: Doubleday & Co., 1974), p. 20.

13. My discussion does not distinguish between "image" and "model." I see these two words used by Dulles and Minear as coterminous.

14. Dulles, *Models of the Church*, p. 23.

15. See Gary MacEoin, ed., "Puebla," *Cross Currents*, vol. 28, no. 1 (Spring 1978), pp. 8–19.

16. Paul Minear, *Images of the Church in the New Testament* (Philadelphia: Westminster Press, 1960), p. 20.

17. Ibid., pp. 22–24.

18. Adolf Harnack, *The Constitution and Law of the Church* (English trans., 1910), pp. 3–5, 257–258.

19. R. Newton Flew, *Jesus and His Church: A Study of the Idea of Ecclesia in the New Testament* (London: Epworth Press, 1960), p. 14.

20. Ibid., p. 182.

Chapter 5: The Holy Spirit and Liberation

1. Compare Eldridge Cleaver's *Soul on Fire* (Waco, Tex.: Word Books, 1978), p. 227, with his *Soul on Ice* (New York: Dell Publishing Co., 1968), pp. 18–25.

2. See Hendrikus Berkhof, *The Doctrine of the Holy Spirit* (Atlanta: John Knox Press, 1976), pop. 13–14.

3. Ibid., pp. 17–18.

4. Pastor Hermas, Similitudo v. 6. 5.

5. Berkhof, *Doctrine*, pp. 19–21.

6. Frederick D. Bruner, *A Theology of the Holy Spirit* (Grand Rapids: Wm. B. Eerdmans Publishing Co., 1970), p. 75.

7. Ibid., p. 282.

8. Ibid., p. 283.

9. Paul D. Opsahl, *The Holy Spirit in the Life of the Church: From Biblical Times to the Present* (Minneapolis: Augsburg Publishing House, 1978).

10. Cf. Erling T. Jorstad, ed., *The Holy Spirit in Today's Church: A Handbook of the New Pentecostalism* (Nashville: Abingdon Press, 1973). See especially pp. 71–76, where "the second blessing" is discussed. This work is comprehensive. It provides varied opinions by Pentecostals and non-Pentecostals in addition to valuable case studies.

11. See Bennie Goodwin, "Social Implications of Pentecostal Power," *Spirit*, vol. 1, no. 1 (1977), pp. 31–35.

12. James S. Tinney, "Exclusivist Tendencies in Pentecostal Self-definition: A Critique from Black Theology," *Journal of Religious Thought*, vol. 36, no. 1 (1979), pp. 32–33. Hereafter cited as *JRT*.

13. Leonard Lovett, "Perspective on the Black Origins of the Contemporary Pentecostal Movement," *JITC*, vol. 1, no. 1 (1973), pp. 39–40, 42.

14. Ibid., p. 41.

15. Tinney, "Exclusivist Tendencies," Cf. his article "William J. Seymour: Father of Modern-Day Pentecostalism," *JRT*, vol. 33, no. 1 (1976), pp. 34–44.

16. Lovett, "Perspective," p. 48.

17. Tinney, "Exclusivist Tendencies," p. 45.

18. James A. Forbes, Jr., "Shall We Call This Dream Progressive Pentecostalism?" *Spirit*, vol. 1, no. 1 (1977), pp. 13–16.

19. Ibid., pp. 14–15.

20. Goodwin, "Social Implications," p. 33.

21. James S. Tinney, "The Blackness of Pentecostalism," *Spirit*, vol. 3, no. 2 (1979), pp. 28–31.

22. Berkhof, *Doctrine*, p. 63.

23. Ibid., pp. 64–65.

24. Major J. Jones, *Black Awareness: A Theology of Hope* (Nashville: Abingdon Press, 1971), pp. 57–58, 100–101.

25. Jürgen Moltmann, *The Church in the Power of the Spirit* (New York: Harper & Row, 1977), p. 198.

26. Samuel Rayan, *The Holy Spirit: Heart of the Gospel and Christian Hope* (Maryknoll, N.Y.: Orbis Books, 1978), p. 137.

Chapter 6: Love as Costly Grace

1. Gerhard Kittel, *Bible Keywords* (New York: Harper & Brothers, 1951), pp. 10–24.

2. Ibid., p. 33.

3. *Bibliotheca Sacra*, vol. 116, no. 463 (July 1959), pp. 241–243.

4. Kittel, *Bible Keywords*, pp. 43–49.

5. Rudolf Bultmann, *Jesus and the Word* (New York: Charles Scribner's Sons, 1958), p. 118.

6. Kittel, *Bible Keywords*, pp. 54–56.

7. Ibid., pp. 61–63.

8. Anders Nygren, *Agape and Eros* (Philadelphia: Westminster Press,

1953), pp. 560, 627, 725. Nygren is a modern opponent of Augustine as well as a vigorous exponent of Luther on the Christian doctrine of love.

Chapter 7: Justice in the Service of Love

1. Gerhard Kittel, *Bible Keywords* (New York: Harper & Brothers, 1951), pp. 10–21.
2. *Encyclopedia of Religion and Ethics*, vol. 10, p. 790.
3. Paul Tillich, *Love, Power, and Justice* (New York: Oxford University Press, 1954), p. 121.
4. Emil Brunner, *Justice and the Social Order* (New York: Harper & Brothers, 1945), pp. 16–17.
5. Ibid., p. 15.
6. Reinhold Niebuhr, *Love and Justice*, ed. by D. B. Robertson (Philadelphia: Westminster Press, 1947), p. 12.
7. G. F. Thomas, *Christian Ethics and Moral Philosophy* (New York: Charles Scribner's Sons, 1935), p. 254.
8. A. C. Knudson, *The Principles of Christian Ethics* (New York: Abingdon-Cokesbury Press, 1943), p. 26.
9. Frederick Herzog, *Justice Church: The New Function of the Church in North American Christianity* (Maryknoll, N.Y.: Orbis Books, 1980), p. 110.
10. Quoted by H. H. Schrey, *The Biblical Doctrine of Justice and Law* (London: SCM Press, 1955), p. 189.

Chapter 8: The Power to Be Human

1. Paul Tillich, *Love, Power, and Justice* (New York: Oxford University Press, 1954), p. 33.
2. Martin Luther King, Jr., *Where Do We Go from Here: Chaos or Community?* (Boston: Beacon Press, 1968), p. 33.
3. Reinhold Niebuhr, *Moral Man and Immoral Society* (New York: Charles Scribner's Sons, 1952).
4. Reinhold Niebuhr, *Christianity and Power Politics* (New York: Charles Scribner's Sons, 1946), pp. 26–27.
5. Niebuhr, *Moral Man and Immoral Society*, p. 234.
6. Niebuhr, *Christianity and Power Politics*, pp. 26–27.
7. Gene Sharp, *The Politics of Nonviolent Action, Part 1: Power and Struggle* (Boston: Porter Sargent Press, 1973), p. 37.
8. King, *Where Do We Go From Here?* p. 129. Both black theology and liberation theology developed after King's death. These theologies together with future events, we can be assured, would have modified King's theological ethics. Unfortunately we cannot indicate how.

Chapter 9: Faith in God Confronts Collective Evils

1. My reading of Gustavo Gutiérrez and other Latin American liberation theologians together with my conversations with Dorothee Soelle, Jürgen Moltmann, and Johannes-Baptist Metz has sharply focused my attention

upon collective evils and mass suffering. The conversation with fellow black theologians as well as African and Asian theologians has made my solidarity with the oppressed more profound. You are invited to examine Johannes-Baptist Metz, *Faith in History and Society: Toward a Practical Fundamental Theology.* tr. by David Smith (New York: Seabury Press, 1980). See especially Part 2, ch. 5, pp. 100–118. Gustavo Gutiérrez, *A Theology of Liberation* (New York: Orbis Books, 1973), is *must* reading.

2. See James H. Cone, *God of the Oppressed* (New York: Seabury Press, 1975), pp. 163–194.

3. We cannot gainsay the crucial importance of those who have helped us to hold on to faith in God in the face of awesome personal suffering. See Arthur C. McGill, *Suffering: A Test of Theological Method* (Philadelphia: Westminster Press, 1982), pp. 112–130. Cf. Rabbi Harold S. Kushner, *When Bad Things Happen to Good People* (New York: Schocken Books, 1981), pp. 113–131.

4. Colin B. Archer, a Bahamian studying in the United States, has written an informed and theologically astute book on the U.S. situation entitled *Poverty: The Church's Abandoned Revolution* (Nassau: Colmar Publications, 1980). See especially chapters 2 and 4 (pp. 6–34 and 44–54).

5. The views expressed here are written elsewhere in greater detail. See my *Roots of the Black Future: Family and Church* (Philadelphia: Westminster Press, 1980) and *Black Theology Today: Liberation and Contextualization,* Toronto Studies in Theology, vol. 12 (Lewiston, N.Y.: Edwin Mellen Press, 1983). The latter work emphasizes political and social theology; see especially pp. 127–178.

Chapter 10: Black Theology in Dialogue: Two Examples

1. The following readings have been helpful in my reflections on Minjung theology: James H. Cone, *A Black Theology of Liberation* (Philadelphia: J. B. Lippincott Co., 1970); Paulo Freire, *Education for Critical Consciousness* (New York: Seabury Press, 1973); Everett N. Hunt, Jr., *Protestant Pioneers in Korea* (Maryknoll, N.Y.: Orbis Books, 1980); Jong-sun Noh, *Religion and Just Revolution: A Third World Perspective* (Hamden, Conn.: Center for Asian Theology, 1984); Kim Yong-Bock et al., ed., *Minjung Theology: People as the Subjects of History* (Maryknoll, N.Y.: Orbis Books, 1983); "From Bangalore to Seoul" (Singapore: A Christian Conference of Asia Report, 1981–1985; hereafter CCA); "Justice and Development" (Singapore: CCA, 1984); "Protestant Christianity in Korea" (Singapore: CCA, 1985); and David Kwang-sun Suh, "Mask Dance of Liberation," CCA (prepared for 8th Assembly, July 2, 1985, Seoul).

2. This dialogue on the religious and theological affinity between Jews and blacks is the result of a request to respond to a paper prepared by Marc Ellis for Theology in the Americas. I was asked to respond from a black theological perspective. The several papers were published in *Doing Theology in the United States,* vol. 1, no. 1, published by Theology in the Americas,

Ellis' paper, pp. 5–17, is entitled "Notes Toward a Jewish Theology of Liberation." My response is found on pp. 23–26 and is repeated here by permission.

Chapter 11: The Future of Black Theology

1. For an informative discussion on contextualization as a theological method, see Douglas Hall, "On Contextuality in Christian Theology," *Toronto Journal of Theology*, vol. 1, part 1 (Spring 1985), pp. 3–16, and Robert McAfee Brown, "What Is Contextual Theology?" in Letty M. Russell, ed., *Changing Contexts of Our Faith* (Philadelphia: Fortress Press, 1985), pp. 80–94. My book *Black Theology Today: Liberation and Contextualization*, Toronto Studies in Theology, vol. 12 (Lewiston, N.Y.: Edwin Mellen Press, 1983), pp. 3–29, outlines somewhat my own perspective on the subject. The present book builds on this initial foundation.

2. See Rosemary Ruether's helpful reflections on this subject; she provides a historical as well as a theological perspective. In *To Change the World* (New York: Crossroad Publishing Co., 1985), pp. 45–56, Ruether engages the question, "Can a Male Savior Save Women?"

3. Richard L. Rubenstein, *The Age of Triage: Fear and Hope in an Overcrowded World* (Boston: Beacon Press, 1983), pp. 1–33.

4. Recent portrayals of the black family have not been constructive, and I am tempted to develop further what has been a key concern of mine, the black family and the church. But I will not do it here. To address appropriately such challenges as the proposed welfare reform of President Reagan, the Moyers Report, or even *The Color Purple* movie would take us far beyond this study.

Index